FAMILY

FAMILY

NEW VEGETARIAN COMFORT FOOD TO NOURISH EVERY DAY

BY HETTY MCKINNON

Photography by Luisa Brimble

PRESTEL

MUNICH · LONDON · NEW YORK

For my mum, for everything.

CONTENTS

INTRODUCTION

Family is our greatest influence in shaping us, in making us.

At the heart of every family, there is a complex story of food. The family table represents a constantly evolving edible history, where nostalgia interlaces with tradition, identity, and culture, and where small moments grow into lasting memories. Along with the food that we eat around the table, there are also the shared experiences—the conversations, reflections, heated discussions, and informal exchanges that add a unique flavor to our food.

Family food isn't fancy or complex. Its roots are humble, stemming from recipes passed on through generations, or food rituals born from daily cooking. At home, even the simplest dish can hold deep significance. It could be a modest fried egg sandwich (which my mother made for me whenever I was cramming for a big exam), a bowl of ginger fried rice (which soothed a sore tummy), or a decorative watermelon basket (which my dad hand-carved for every childhood birthday party) that reminds us of a time, a person, or a feeling. The food we ate as children comforts us because it is evocative of a time when we were happy or nurtured; it connects us to our past, and provides a pathway to our future.

Family ties

This book is rooted at home, and observes how our families influence who we are and what we eat. Sharing food together around the table is the most basic act of kinship, but its effects are far-reaching and consequential. The table is a unifier—when we converse with one another around food, ideas are sparked, creativity is kindled, characters are formed, and lifelong habits are engendered.

Wherever I am in the world, it is the culinary foundations of my mother's dining table that influence and inspire me the most. Food was an intensely serious affair in our house. I would wake to my mother standing over her wok and go to sleep with her organizing the kitchen for the next day. Our dinners typically consisted of five or six Cantonese dishes served alongside a medicinal broth—not always our favorite—and rice. My mother didn't drive, so she would take multiple buses or trains just to purchase the best brand of tofu or noodles. But even so, it is not her delicious food or her audacious approach to feeding that inspires me most. Rather, it is her intent. For her, cooking was her way of nurturing. In our home, as it is in many Asian families, food was a means of communication, enabling our parents to convey their feelings towards their children. Traditionally, it is rare for Asian parents to verbally express their love for their children; rather, they *show* their affection through feeding them delicious—and often copious amounts of—food.

While I am a mother who is very different culturally to the one I grew up with, it is my mum's love of feeding that fuels me. It is the very life force that pumps through my veins. Within my own busy family life, prioritizing the life force of mealtimes is paramount—this is a time when we can engage with one another with intent and consideration, building a sense of belonging and strengthening our own family ties.

NEW FAMILY CLASSICS

Dreaming up flavorful yet nutritious meals, night after night, is one of the greatest challenges in cooking for your family. It's even harder to think of meals that incorporate plenty of vegetables. My mother would often say that "thinking" of a dish to cook was much harder than actually making it; I wholeheartedly agree.

Family meals should not be a chore, although I know they can often feel this way. Over the years, I have learned that cooking for your family is made easier by drawing on "classics"—meals that we can pull together from memory with minimal effort and ingredients. For me, developing a "repertoire" is the key—these are the dishes that you can shop for without a list, that are adaptable, that you can cook consistently with aplomb, and serve time after time to an appreciative audience.

The recipes in this book are my new family classics, the multicultural meals that I like to serve around my table. Some are old favorites, and many are variations on much-loved comfort food, repackaged with a healthier outlook.

We all have our own way of choosing what to cook, but for me, I like to start off with a "type of dish." Do I feel like salad or am I craving a warming baked dish today? At least once a week, sometimes twice, nothing else but an Asian dish will do. Some days, I yearn for a huge bowl of veg-laden soup, or often I hunger for eggs. And of course, pasta night— what would we do without pasta night? These are the types of dishes I serve up most frequently at my table and they are a good place to start building your own repertoire.

HOW TO EAT GREEN, TOGETHER

At the heart of *Family* is creating food that the whole family can enjoy, together. If your family isn't fully vegetarian, like mine, it can be a challenge to create vegetable-heavy dishes that are satisfying to all culinary sensibilities, especially those of younger children. *Family*, like my two previous books, vehemently moves away from the idea that vegetables cannot be a full-size meal. In this book, I venture deeper into family life, offering recipes and tips that will—hopefully!—tempt everyone around the table, young and old, to eat green.

As a child, I don't remember my mum ever telling us to "eat your vegetables." We ate our greens with the same enthusiasm as we ate our noodles, rice, or meat. In Asian cooking, as in many other cultures, vegetables are an integral part of the dish, not a sideshow. Think lettuce braised with mushrooms, tomato stewed with eggs, and broccoli served with noodles—there were no hunks of meat surrounded by three vegetables at our table. Inspired by the way we ate as kids, the recipes in this book aim to present vegetables as a cohesive part of a delicious, comforting dish.

Over the years, I have thought a lot about how to present vegetarian food to my family in a way that is familiar and flavorful. You may notice that the recipes in this book feature less herbs than my usual herbaceous style—recently, I discovered that my kids (and many adults, too) don't love herbs as much as I do (how horrific, right?)! There are certain herbs that are usually well received—basil, parsley, mint, and thyme. Then there are the tolerated herbs—chives, shallots, and rosemary. And then there is the ultimate divisive herb—cilantro. Using less herbs in my vegetarian dishes, or sometimes in cunning ways where they are hidden in a sauce or dressing, has revolutionized mealtimes in our house. My kids are now devouring plant-packed meals that they previously deplored. This herbal discovery, along with the little tips and tricks below, has made our family mealtimes greener and happier.

- Present everyday vegetables in a comforting way—add some spinach, cauliflower, or sweet potato to family favorites like macaroni and cheese, mashed potatoes, or lasagna.

- Add complexity to your vegetables with gentle spices such as ground coriander and cumin. Introduce spices early on to acquaint young palates with different flavors.

- Tread carefully with herbs—don't add too many—and try to find the ones that your kids like (basil and mint tend to be kid faves). Serve the herbs on the side and encourage them to add as much or as little as they like.

- Many people prefer their vegetables raw because of the crunchy texture. Vegetables like fennel, asparagus, broccoli, or thinly shaved beets are often preferred raw by the young ones.

- Pair the vegetable with an ingredient that you know your kids will like. A big plate of vegetables can feel threatening to some, so try adding croutons, sliced avocado, hard-boiled eggs, or Parmesan shavings.

- Try different varieties of vegetables. My kids don't love the strong flavor of button or cremini mushrooms, but they don't mind the more mellow flavors of shiitake.

- If you don't succeed with a dish the first time, try again later. Palates change constantly and often need time to "get used to" a texture or flavor.

THE FAMILY PANTRY

The family pantry is the engine of your kitchen. When it is well stocked, it will keep your daily cooking whirring, churning out satisfying and healthy meals for the family.

Family is a book celebrating humble everyday ingredients. The ingredients are easy to find in your local supermarket or greengrocer. And if you can't find a specific item, substitute it with another. It's okay. Learn to be flexible in the kitchen.

Building a family pantry takes time and patience. Add spices and ingredients gradually. If you are shopping for canned, frozen, or dry ingredients, buy two instead of one, and stash the spare in the pantry for a rainy day. Each week, purchase a packet of pasta or noodles as these will always get eaten.

Don't forget your freezer—it is an essential pantry space, perfect for keeping cooking building blocks such as frozen vegetables; pre-cooked grains such as quinoa, pearl barley or farro; surplus herbs and aromatics such as shallots, chiles, and ginger; and leftover sauces such as pesto and tomato-based pasta sauces.

The following pantry list includes most of the ingredients used in this book, apart from fresh fruit and vegetables. It may seem extensive, but most of these are basic and inexpensive pantry ingredients that are useful in everyday cooking.

In the cupboard

Breadcrumbs (regular and panko)
Canned beans (chickpeas, cannellini, borlotti, butter beans)
Canned tomatoes (puréed, diced, whole, passata)
Coconut (unsweetened shredded)
Coconut cream or milk
Cooking chocolate
Cornstarch
Cornmeal
Couscous (regular and Israeli, or pearl)
Croutons (store-bought or made from stale bread)
Dried shiitake mushrooms
Flour (all-purpose and self-rising)
Lentils (green, black, Puy)
Noodles (soba, ramen, rice vermicelli, mung bean vermicelli)
Peanut butter
Pearl barley
Quick-cooking polenta or store-bought pre-cooked polenta
Quinoa
Rice (white, brown, basmati)
Seaweed (hijiki, kombu, nori, wakame)
Sugar (superfine and brown)
Tahini
Thai curry paste

Nuts and seeds (toasted)

Almonds (slivered and sliced)
Dukkah mix (homemade or store-bought)
Peanuts
Pecans
Pine nuts
Poppy seeds
Pumpkin seeds
Sesame seeds (white and black)
Sunflower seeds
Walnuts

Sauces and condiments

Good-quality vegetable stock powder
Mirin
Sesame oil
Tamari (gluten free) or soy sauce
Vegetarian oyster sauce
Vinegar (white wine, red wine, apple cider, rice wine, balsamic, white balsamic, sherry)

Spices

Bay leaves
Cayenne pepper
Cinnamon (ground and sticks)
Coriander (ground and seeds)
Cumin (ground and seeds)
Dried chiles (regular and chipotle)
Dried mint
Dried oregano
Fennel seeds
Ground turmeric
Paprika (sweet or smoked)
Red chile flakes
Star anise
Szechuan peppercorns

In the freezer

Corn
Edamame
Peas
Spinach

In the fridge

Butter
Capers
Cornichons or gherkins
Eggs
Feta
Greek yogurt or créme fraîche
Kimchi
Lemons
Limes
Maple syrup
Miso paste
Mustard (Dijon)
Olives (black wrinkly, kalamata, green)
Parmesan cheese
Tomato paste
Good-quality mayonnaise

On the counter

Alliums (garlic, onions, shallots)
Black pepper
Maldon sea salt
Olive oil (regular and extra-virgin)
Vegetable or sunflower oil

MIDWEEK CHEATS

The cooking of daily meals can be as simple or as complicated as your life allows it to be. Even if you only have 10 minutes to cook a meal, give that 10 minutes your all! A genius weeknight dinner can be made with the scantiest of ingredients—team a single roasted or raw vegetable with a canned legume or grain, and dress it in an herby oil. If you scatter over some nuts or seeds, you have yourself a relatively fancy salad. If you throw an egg on top, you have a big hearty plate.

The transformative element of vegetable-based dishes is often the sauce, which brings cohesion to the final dish. While I generally love complex sauces, during the week, I often call upon two very basic sauces, or "cheat dressings" as I call them, to add life to vegetable dishes.

Chunky herb oil

Makes about ½ cup

This sauce could be made with a mortar and pestle, but when I'm particularly lazy, I just use a sharp knife and a cutting board.

½–1 bunch of soft herbs (parsley, dill, cilantro,
    basil, mint, scallions etc.)
1 small garlic clove
big pinch of sea salt
¼–⅓ cup (60–80 ml) extra-virgin olive oil

Place the herbs on a cutting board and layer on the garlic and salt. Bunch everything together and begin chopping finely, until the herbs and garlic are mashed together. Place in small bowl, cover with olive oil, and stir.

Best served with

broccoli and pasta
brown rice or grain bowls
cannellini beans
charred zucchini and quinoa
roasted or boiled potatoes
roasted or shaved brussels sprouts
shaved fennel

Citrus tahini

Makes about ½ cup

3 tablespoons tahini
1 small garlic clove, very finely chopped
juice of ½–1 lemon or lime
sea salt

Place the tahini in a small bowl and add the garlic and citrus juice. Slowly drizzle in some water and whisk together, then continue drizzling in water until the tahini is the consistency of cream (if the mixture seizes and becomes too thick to stir, add more water until it smooths out). Season with sea salt.

Best served with

brown rice or grain bowls
raw slaw of cabbage, beet, and carrot
roasted carrots with chickpeas
roasted cauliflower
roasted or charred eggplant
roasted sweet potato

THE MAGIC OF BEANS

If I have a can of beans on hand, I feel empowered in the kitchen. Pre-cooked beans are one of the most versatile pantry ingredients for successful daily cooking. They are the foundation of so many hurried meals in my house. One humble can of beans delivers so many spectacular meal options.

Six ways with a can of beans

Fry them
Throw your drained beans into a frying pan, add some good glugs of olive oil, a little very finely chopped garlic and a few essential spices—try cumin, paprika, smoked paprika, chile, cayenne, turmeric, or fennel seeds. Fry until crispy. Eat as a snack or serve with roasted or chargrilled vegetables.

Pesto them
Beans are excellent in a pesto-like sauce. Replace the nuts or seeds with spoonfuls of beans. Add drained beans, basil, garlic, and sea salt and whiz it all up for a creamy, very unpesto-like pesto. Stir in some grated Parmesan, if you desire.

Roast them
Here is a simple formula for the most irresistibly crunchy beans—drain a can of beans, place in a small ovenproof dish, drizzle with enough oil to almost cover, add as much garlic as you are comfortable with, salt it, add a few spices such as cumin and paprika, and roast in a blazing hot oven until the beans are crispy on top. It should take about 20 minutes in a hot oven.

Sandwich them
White beans such as cannellini or navy beans make a perfect open sandwich topping. Add some drained beans to a pan along with a good amount of olive oil, one or two very finely chopped garlic cloves, a sprig of rosemary, sage, or thyme and about ½ cup (125 ml) of vegetable stock or water, and simmer until thickened up. Season with sea salt and black pepper. Serve it on top of some crusty ciabatta or sourdough bread and sprinkle with red chile flakes.

Smash them
Best made using a mortar and pestle, smash up your drained beans with a small clove of garlic, a hit of spices such as cumin, coriander, or paprika, and drizzle with enough oil to make it pleasantly chunky. Toss this smashed goodness with some of your favorite roasted veggies.

Soup them
A simple bean soup is as easy as tossing your drained beans into a pan, adding a little vegetable stock, perhaps a can of tomatoes, and maybe a bunch of greens, and simmering it until you extract some wonderful flavors. If you want a smooth soup, blend it up.

"COMPOST" VEGETABLE STOCK

Most days of the week, I use a store-bought vegetable stock powder. My favorite brand is the one my mum always uses—Vegeta Gourmet Stock Powder—and it is readily available everywhere. She adds it to everything, even her meat dishes, to "bring out the flavor." At other times, it is fun to make a vegetable stock from scratch, using kitchen scraps. Using just three basic ingredients as its foundation—onion, celery, and carrots—this stock is made with your vegetable trimmings. Carrot peel, celery leaves, mushroom stems, herb stems, onion skin, shallot and leek ends, and wilted greens and herbs are excellent flavorings for your stock. You can even freeze them in batches and grab them when the stock-making need hits. Just make sure that your scraps are clean and avoid cruciferous veggies, such as cabbage, broccoli, cauliflower, and Brussels sprouts, as they can leave a bitter flavor.

Things to add for flavor

- Bay leaf
- Dried shiitake mushrooms: My mum adds these to all her soup bases for unbelievable flavor. Have a packet on hand in your pantry. As they are dried, they have a long shelf life and you can just grab a few when you need them.
- Fresh ginger
- Garlic cloves
- Peppercorns
- Seaweed: A sheet of kombu, wakame, or kelp adds an incredible umami taste to your stock. This is my essential stock ingredient.

"Compost" vegetable stock

Makes about 8 cups (2 liters)

extra-virgin olive oil
4 garlic cloves, peeled
2 onions, chopped
2–3 carrots, roughly chopped
4 celery stalks, chopped
3–4 cups (600–800 g) vegetable scraps
1 seaweed sheet
sea salt

OPTIONAL FLAVORINGS
4 black or white peppercorns
2 bay leaves
2 dried shiitake mushrooms
ginger, peeled and sliced
herbs: parsley, thyme, cilantro, sage, rosemary

Place a stockpot or Dutch oven over a medium heat. Add a drizzle of oil and toss in the garlic, onion, carrot, and celery. Cook for 4–5 minutes, until the veggies are starting to soften. Add 10–12 cups (2.5–3 liters) of water, along with the vegetable scraps, the seaweed sheet, and any of your optional flavorings, season with sea salt, and bring to the boil. Reduce the heat, cover, and simmer for 1 hour.

Strain the stock through a mesh sieve or fine colander.

Store in an airtight jar or container in the fridge for up to 1 week. Or you can freeze for 6 months (or even longer). Think about freezing in smaller portions of 2–3 cups (500–750 ml), so you can defrost what you need.

RECIPE NOTES

Cup and spoon measurements for herbs and greens (such as arugula, baby spinach, etc.) are always tightly packed. Most of the time, the recipes in this book are written to be flexible regarding the amount of herbs used. Use as much as you desire. For sauces and dressings, I have supplied more specific herb measurements to help you achieve flavor balance.

For parsley, flat-leaf is preferred but not mandatory. Curly parsley is also fine.

I always use Maldon sea salt for seasoning. For flavoring your cooking water, use a regular sea salt or cooking salt.

Black pepper is better freshly ground.

I generally use extra-virgin olive oil for everyday cooking. For high-temperature cooking, choose a neutral oil such as sunflower, vegetable, safflower, canola, or grapeseed oil.

For eggs, use the freshest you can find. Free range is great, free range and organic is even better, or straight from the farm (or your yard) if you're lucky.

Cooking times will vary depending upon the oven you are using. The temperatures given in this book are for a conventional oven, which can be up to 68°F (20°C) lower than a convection oven. Know your oven and adjust temperatures and cooking times according to your needs.

SALAD

DAYS

SALADS ARE ADVENTURE.

Salads are the pioneers of the food world. They are bold, restless, dauntless, and vivid, never shirking an opportunity to venture to a new place. From the leafy garden vegetables of the first century to the Waldorf salad of the late 1800s, and the Caesar and Cobb salads of the 1920s, salads have evolved into a sophisticated, worldly dish. No longer a side dish, full-bodied main meal salads are now a major food attraction, featuring diverse ingredients and intriguing textures. With a single vegetable at the helm, salads now journey to the most far-flung corners of the globe with just the addition of a spice, an herb, a nut, a seed, or a sauce. In our home, salads are the meals that spark endless conversation around the table. Never underestimate the power of a salad to deliver a hearty, deeply gratifying meal to the whole family. There is no better dish to bring people together. Salad days are every day.

ROASTED CAULIFLOWER WITH PEAS AND MINT-PEA YOGURT

Serves 4 / gluten free

In our house, roasted cauliflower is highly sought after. We eat it two or three times a week, often on its own, sometimes sprinkled with pomegranate seeds, and occasionally dressed up in a punchy sauce. This herbaceous yogurt has loads of attitude—vibrantly green with the addition of peas, this sweet minty sauce is also lovely as a creamy pasta sauce.

1 cauliflower head (1¾ pounds/about 800 g), cut into large florets
extra-virgin olive oil
1 cup (200 g) quinoa, rinsed
2 cups (500 ml) vegetable stock or water
2 cups (250 g) frozen peas
1 cup (90 g) bean sprouts or microgreens
¼ cup (6 g) mint leaves
sea salt and black pepper

MINT-PEA YOGURT

½ cup (80 g) frozen peas
¼ cup (6 g) mint leaves, roughly chopped
1 cup (250 g) Greek yogurt
1 tablespoon extra-virgin olive oil
1 teaspoon maple syrup or honey
sea salt and black pepper

Substitute

frozen peas: fresh peas

quinoa: grains such as pearl barley, farro, freekeh, brown rice

Preheat the oven to 400°F (200°C).

Place the cauliflower florets on a baking sheet and drizzle with olive oil. Roast for 20–25 minutes, until tender and golden. Remove from the oven and season with sea salt and black pepper.

Add the quinoa to a saucepan and pour over the vegetable stock or water. Bring to the boil, then cover, reduce the heat to low, and cook for 15–20 minutes, until the quinoa is translucent and has absorbed all the liquid. Remove from the heat and allow to cool for 5–10 minutes in the pan. Fluff with a fork.

Bring a small pot of well-salted water to the boil. Blanch the peas—including the peas for the yogurt sauce—for 60 seconds. Drain and refresh under cold running water until completely cold. Set aside.

To make the mint-pea yogurt, combine the mint, ½ cup (80 g) of the blanched peas, and the yogurt in a blender or food processor and blend until smooth. Add the olive oil and maple syrup or honey, season with sea salt and black pepper, and blend until everything is combined.

Combine the cauliflower, quinoa, and peas, drizzle with some olive oil, and season with sea salt and black pepper. To serve, dollop the pea yogurt all over the cauliflower and top with sprouts or microgreens and mint leaves.

GRAIN BOWL WITH CRISPY BRUSSELS SPROUTS AND SAUCE GRIBICHE

Serves 4–6

A salad dressing made of eggs is *some kind of wonderful*. Sauce *gribiche* is a masterful French concoction, similar to mayonnaise, but using cooked egg yolk rather than raw. It is savory and tart, a daring balance of acid and fat that is brightened with the addition of cornichons and capers. The French like to serve sauce gribiche with veal head, but I will settle for a grain bowl. It's a lively sauce that is amazing served with just about any roasted vegetables, particularly crispy potatoes, asparagus, or even straight up, on a piece of toast.

1½ cups (330 g) pearl barley or farro
4 cups (1 liter) vegetable stock
extra-virgin olive oil
1 pound (450 g) Brussels sprouts, trimmed and quartered
2 handfuls of baby spinach leaves
1 tablespoon chopped chives
juice of ½ small lemon
sea salt and black pepper

SAUCE GRIBICHE

3 hard-boiled large eggs, peeled
2 teaspoons Dijon mustard
⅓ cup (80 ml) extra-virgin olive oil
2 teaspoons red wine vinegar
1 tablespoon capers, rinsed and roughly chopped
6 tiny cornichons or 1 small gherkin, finely chopped
1 tablespoon chopped flat-leaf parsley leaves
sea salt and black pepper

Substitute

Brussels sprouts: broccoli, kale, asparagus, cauliflower, potato

Rinse your chosen grains and place them in a saucepan set over a medium heat. Cover with the stock, bring to the boil, and cook for 20–25 minutes, until the grains are tender. Drain.

Make the sauce gribiche by removing the egg yolks from the boiled eggs. Chop the egg whites into small cubes and set aside. Mash the yolks together with the Dijon mustard in a bowl. Drizzle in the olive oil and whisk together until emulsified, then slowly stir in the vinegar until well combined. Add the capers, cornichon or gherkin, chopped egg whites, and parsley. Season with sea salt and a good turn of black pepper. Taste and adjust the salt, pepper, and vinegar if necessary.

Heat a large frying pan over a medium heat, add a good drizzle of olive oil, and toss in the Brussels sprouts. Season with a pinch of sea salt and cook for 3–4 minutes, tossing the pan often to avoid burning, until the sprouts are crispy and tender.

To serve, place the grains in a serving bowl and add the spinach leaves, Brussels sprouts, and chives. Season everything with sea salt, black pepper, a squeeze of lemon juice, and a drizzle of olive oil. Toss together gently and spoon over the sauce gribiche to finish.

TIPS

The sauce gribiche can be made 2 days ahead and stored in the fridge. You can also use other herbs such as dill, chives, and chervil, and you can replace the vinegar with lemon juice.

If you like your Brussels sprouts extra crispy, you can deep-fry them.

Farro or pearl barley can be made ahead and chilled in the fridge for 2 days. It can also be frozen.

GNOCCHI WITH ASPARAGUS, EDAMAME, AND PARMESAN

Serves 4

This salad of humble ingredients was inspired by a dish we enjoyed at a fine dining restaurant in Sydney, eons ago. The cute neighborhood bistro is long gone, but the memory of this dish prevails. The gnocchi served at the restaurant was freshly made, but for my home-style dish, I go for everyday vacuum-packed or frozen gnocchi. Pan-fried gnocchi can almost pass for roast potato—crispy on the outside, chewy on the inside— and is just wonderful in this fun family salad.

1 pound (450 g) store-bought potato
    gnocchi
extra-virgin olive oil
1 large bunch of asparagus
    (1 pound/450 g), woody stems
    removed, cut into 2-inch (5 cm) pieces
1 cup (150 g) frozen shelled
    edamame beans
1 tablespoon chopped chives
juice of 1 small lemon
2 ounces (60 g) Parmesan, shaved
sea salt and black pepper

Substitute

gnocchi: new or fingerling potatoes
(for gluten free)

Bring a large pot of salted water to the boil and add the gnocchi. Cook for 2–3 minutes, until the gnocchi float to the top. Drain and refresh under cold running water.

Heat a large frying pan over a medium–high heat, drizzle with oil, and, once hot, add the asparagus, along with a pinch of sea salt. Fry for about 2 minutes, until the asparagus pieces are starting to char but are still crisp. Remove from the pan.

Place the pan back on the heat and add the frozen edamame together with a splash of water and a pinch of sea salt. Cook for 2–3 minutes, until the beans are soft yet still have a bite. Drain and add to the asparagus.

In the same pan over a medium–high heat, drizzle some oil and, when hot, add the gnocchi. Fry until the gnocchi are golden and crispy. Remove from the pan and allow everything to cool slightly.

Combine the gnocchi with the asparagus, edamame, and chives. Squeeze over the lemon juice, drizzle over some olive oil, and season with a big pinch of sea salt and lots of black pepper. To serve, place the salad on a serving plate and scatter over the shaved Parmesan.

SMASHED PEAS WITH FREEKEH, BROCCOLI, AND AVOCADO

Serves 4

Peas, and frozen ones too, are compelling protagonists in family cooking: inexpensive, accessible, and requiring minimal preparation. It doesn't hurt to keep one or two—or three!—bags in your freezer for every occasion. These smashed peas are a fine example of how satisfying and flavorful everyday ingredients can be; in this salad, they bring an exciting green creaminess to the vegetables and grains. The smashed peas can also be used as a chunky pasta sauce, especially when served with a small pasta shape, such as orecchiette.

1 large broccoli head
   (about 1 pound/450 g),
   cut into florets
extra-virgin olive oil
1 cup (250 g) freekeh, rinsed
3 cups (750 ml) vegetable stock or water
1 avocado
1 handful of baby spinach leaves
1 radish, thinly sliced
½ cup (75 g) feta, cubed
2 tablespoons slivered almonds, toasted
sea salt and black pepper

SMASHED PEAS

2 cups (310 g) frozen peas
1 garlic clove, finely chopped
½ cup (12 g) basil leaves, finely chopped
2 tablespoons extra-virgin olive oil
juice of ½ lemon
sea salt and black pepper

Substitute

freekeh: quinoa (for gluten free)

Heat a grill pan or grill until it is very hot. Place the broccoli florets in a bowl and drizzle with olive oil. Cook the broccoli on the hot pan or grill for 3–4 minutes, turning often to achieve an even char. Set aside.

Add the freekeh to a saucepan and pour over the vegetable stock or water. Bring to the boil, then cover, reduce the heat to low, and cook for 20–25 minutes, until the freekeh is tender. Drain and set aside.

To make the smashed peas, bring a small pot of salted water to the boil, add the peas, and blanch for 2 minutes. Drain immediately, reserving 2–3 tablespoons of the cooking liquid for the mashing, and rinse under cold running water until the peas are completely cold. Place the cold peas, garlic, and basil in a food processor or blender and pulse four or five times to break up the peas. Add the reserved pea cooking liquid, olive oil, and lemon juice and pulse again a few times until combined, but still quite chunky. (You can also pound this mixture together using a mortar and pestle.) Season with sea salt and black pepper.

Peel the avocado and chop into large chunks.

Combine the broccoli, freekeh, avocado, and spinach with half of the smashed peas and a drizzle of olive oil. Season with sea salt and black pepper and toss to combine. Place the salad on a serving plate and spoon over more of the smashed peas. Scatter over the radish slices, feta, and toasted almonds.

TIPS

Leftover smashed peas can be stored in an airtight container and frozen for up to 3 months.

Smashed peas can also be served as a dip or spread on a slice of bread.

ROAST POTATOES WITH LENTILS, CAPERS, AND LEMON—PARSLEY PISTOU

Serves 4 / gluten free / vegan

Pistou is not to be confused with pesto, though it can be used in a similar way. Pistou hails from the south of France, and is a mélange of fresh basil, garlic, and oil. Traditionally, it is made by hand with a mortar and pestle, so I encourage you to do the same—though you can absolutely whiz it all up in a blender to save time and energy. Potatoes, laced with lemon and parsley, are a wonderful thing.

2 ¼ pounds (1 kg) fingerling or new
  potatoes, peeled and halved
extra-virgin olive oil
1 cup (185 g) green lentils, rinsed
1 tablespoon capers, rinsed, patted dry,
  and roughly chopped
3 tablespoons pine nuts, toasted
handful of parsley leaves
sea salt and black pepper

LEMON—PARSLEY PISTOU
½ cup (12 g) parsley leaves, roughly
  chopped
1 garlic clove, chopped
zest and juice of ½ lemon, plus extra
  if needed
⅓ cup (80 ml) extra-virgin olive oil
sea salt

Preheat the oven to 425°F (220°C).

Place the potato pieces on a large baking sheet and drizzle over some olive oil. Season with sea salt and black pepper. Roast in the hot oven for 30–35 minutes, until the potatoes are golden and tender.

Meanwhile, place the lentils in a pot, cover with plenty of water, and bring to the boil. Add 2 big pinches of salt, reduce the heat to low, and simmer for 15–20 minutes, until the lentils are just soft. Drain and set aside.

To make the pistou, using a mortar and pestle, pound the parsley and garlic together with a pinch of salt until the mixture resembles a paste. Stir in the lemon zest and juice, then slowly drizzle in the oil, stirring continuously. Season with sea salt and adjust the oil and lemon juice to strike the right zesty balance.

When the potatoes are ready and still warm, place them in a large bowl and add the lentils and capers. Add 2 tablespoons of the pistou and toss through to coat.

Transfer the salad to a serving plate and spoon over the rest of the pistou. To serve, scatter over the pine nuts and parsley.

SUPERCHARGED KALE PANZANELLA
WITH POLENTA CROUTONS

Serves 4 / gluten free

Panzanella is a fantastic peasant-style dish thrown together with ripe tomatoes and croutons made from stale bread. This version is supercharged, with the addition of nutrient-rich kale and sunflower seeds. If you are short on time, simply dress in olive oil and balsamic vinegar, but if you have a spare 5 minutes, whiz up this healthy kale pesto. The polenta croutons—thanks to my friend Jill Fergus for the idea!—are a great alternative to traditional croutons, but if you prefer, use regular croutons, either homemade or store-bought.

½ bunch of kale, stems removed
extra-virgin olive oil
3½ ounces (100 g) tomatoes, cut into chunks
9 ounces (250 g) fresh mozzarella or bocconcini, roughly torn
2 tablespoons sunflower seeds, toasted
1 tablespoon grated Parmesan
sea salt and black pepper

KALE AND BASIL PESTO

½ bunch of kale, stems removed
¼ cup (6 g) basil leaves
3 tablespoons sunflower seeds
½ cup (125 ml) extra-virgin olive oil
⅓ cup (50 g) grated Parmesan
2 teaspoons red wine vinegar
sea salt

POLENTA CROUTONS

extra-virgin olive oil
1 pound (450 g) store-bought pre-cooked polenta, cut into ½-inch (1 cm) cubes
sea salt

Substitute

polenta: bread croutons

For the polenta croutons, heat a large frying pan over a high heat. When hot, drizzle with a big glug of oil and add the polenta cubes. Fry for 5–6 minutes, until golden and crispy on all sides. Season with sea salt and set aside to cool completely.

For the salad, tear up the kale leaves and place them in a large bowl. Add a drizzle of olive oil and a pinch of salt and massage them into the leaves. Set aside for 10 minutes to allow the leaves to soften.

To make the pesto, place the kale and basil in a food processor or blender. Pulse to break up the leaves. Add the sunflower seeds and pulse again, then add the oil and blend together until you get a thick yet slightly chunky paste. Pour into a small bowl and stir in the Parmesan and vinegar. Season well with sea salt.

Combine the softened kale leaves with the tomato, mozzarella or bocconcini, sunflower seeds, and Parmesan. Add a few spoonfuls of the pesto and toss well to coat the leaves. To serve, season with sea salt and black pepper and scatter over the polenta croutons.

TIP

You won't need all the pesto. Place the remaining pesto in an airtight container or resealable freezer bag and freeze for up to 3 months.

THE DECONSTRUCTED FALAFEL SALAD

Serves 4 / vegan

Falafels are the perfect plant-based morsel and a family favorite. However, in this salad, I've dismantled perfection and discovered a new, delicious way to enjoy the feted flavors of falafels—chickpeas, cumin, parsley, mint, and tahini. The crispy oven-roasted chickpeas are nothing short of incredible, and I encourage you to try roasting all types of beans in this manner.

extra-virgin olive oil
2 bunches of kale, stems removed
    and leaves torn
1 Persian cucumber, sliced into
    thin rounds
3 cups (150 g) store-bought pita chips
handful of flat-leaf parsley leaves,
    roughly chopped
handful of mint leaves
1 lemon, cut into wedges
sea salt

CRISPY ROASTED CHICKPEAS

18 ounces (500 g) cooked chickpeas
    (about 2 drained cans), patted dry
extra-virgin olive oil
2 garlic cloves, finely chopped
2 teaspoons ground cumin
1 teaspoon paprika
sea salt and black pepper

LEMON TAHINI

⅓ cup (90 g) tahini
juice of 1 lemon, plus extra if needed
1 garlic clove, very finely chopped
sea salt and black pepper

Substitute

chickpeas: white beans, butter beans
omit pita chips for gluten free

Preheat the oven to 425°F (220°C).

For the crispy roasted chickpeas, place the drained chickpeas in a small ovenproof dish. Cover with olive oil, season well with two big pinches of sea salt and black pepper, and add the garlic, cumin, and paprika. Stir to combine. Roast for 35–40 minutes, until the chickpeas are crispy. Set aside.

For the salad, place a large frying pan over a medium heat and drizzle with oil. Add the kale, in batches, along with a pinch of salt and cook for 2–3 minutes, until wilted.

To make the lemon tahini, pour the tahini into a small bowl and whisk in the lemon juice and garlic. Gradually add 1 tablespoon of water at a time, until the sauce is the consistency of thickened cream. If the tahini "seizes" and becomes very thick, add more water; it will eventually come back together to form a cohesive creamy sauce. Season with sea salt and black pepper, and add more lemon juice if you like it lemony.

Combine the crispy chickpeas (and their cooking oil) with the kale, cucumber, half the pita chips and herbs. To serve, drizzle over the lemon tahini and scatter over the remaining pita chips. Serve with lemon wedges on the side.

CHARRED GREEK SALAD WITH FETA AND MINT DRESSING

Serves 4–6

This dish is an interpretation of the inimitable Greek salad, but is a little richer with the addition of charred cucumbers, tomatoes, and lemons. The feta cheese dressing is perfectly smoky and salty, and with its heavy mint notes, it makes this dish shine. The cooked cucumbers are a revelation, evocative of many Asian dishes we enjoyed as kids—my mum cooked them as she would any Asian marrow or gourd, in hot soups and stir-fries.

14 ounces (400 g) Persian cucumbers, halved lengthwise
1 pound (450 g) tomatoes, cut into large chunks
1 lemon, halved
2 thyme sprigs, leaves picked
extra-virgin olive oil
1½ cups (300 g) orzo pasta
½ cup (90 g) kalamata olives, pitted
handful of flat-leaf parsley leaves, finely chopped
sea salt and black pepper

FETA AND MINT DRESSING

1 cup (150 g) Greek feta cheese, crumbled
2–3 teaspoons extra-virgin olive oil
⅓ cup (9 g) mint leaves, finely chopped
½ teaspoon dried mint leaves
juice of ½ lemon
1 small garlic clove, very finely chopped
black pepper

Substitute

cucumbers: zucchini

orzo: brown rice or quinoa (both gluten free)

Place the cucumbers, tomatoes, and lemon in a bowl and add the thyme, a drizzle of olive oil, and a pinch of sea salt. Toss well to coat.

Heat a grill pan or grill until searing hot, add the cucumbers, tomatoes, and lemon, cut-side down, and leave to char for 2–3 minutes. When charred, remove and set aside in a bowl to cool. Remove the lemon and set aside for later.

When the cucumber halves are cool enough to handle, cut them diagonally into thick slices and return them to the bowl with the tomatoes. Season everything with a pinch of sea salt and black pepper.

Bring a large pot of salted water to the boil and add the orzo. Cook for 10 minutes, until the orzo is al dente. Drain and refresh under cold running water.

To make the dressing, place the feta in a small bowl and add the olive oil, fresh and dried mint, lemon juice, and garlic. Season with black pepper. Stir to break up the feta and create a chunky sauce.

Combine the orzo, cucumber, tomato, olives, and parsley. Add half the dressing and toss to combine. Transfer to a serving plate, season with sea salt and black pepper, and spoon over the remaining dressing. Serve with the charred lemon on the side.

GRILLED CORN SALAD WITH SESAME-CRUSTED AVOCADO, COUSCOUS, AND LIME CREMA

Serves 4–6

Grilling corn on the barbecue imparts a lovely smoky sweetness that my family just adores (and if you don't have a grill, you can also cook it on the stovetop using a grill pan or normal frying pan). The sesame- encrusted avocado is nutty and creamy and pairs so well with the zesty lime crema. Cooking avocado does bring out a much stronger flavor, so if that's not for you, skip the frying and enjoy it raw.

3 corn cobs, husks removed
extra-virgin olive oil
3 tablespoons (40 g) sesame seeds (white, black, or both), toasted
1 large (or 2 small) avocado, halved, pitted, and peeled
1½ cups (280 g) couscous
2 cups (500 ml) just-boiled vegetable stock
2 big handfuls of baby arugula leaves
handful of cilantro leaves (optional)
sea salt and black pepper

LIME CREMA
½ cup (125 g) crème fraîche
zest and juice of 1 lime
½ garlic clove, very finely chopped
sea salt

Substitute
couscous: quinoa (for gluten free)

To make the lime crema, place the crème fraîche in a small bowl and add the lime zest and juice and the garlic. Stir to combine and season with sea salt. Set aside.

Preheat a grill, grill pan, or large frying pan to high. Coat the corn in olive oil, place it on the hot cooking surface, and cook, turning often, until evenly charred on all sides. Remove and allow to cool. When cool enough to handle, slice one cob into ½-inch (1 cm) thick slices and, using a sharp knife, remove the kernels from the other two cobs. Set aside.

Place the sesame seeds in a shallow bowl and season with sea salt and black pepper. Slice each avocado half into four wedges. Carefully dip each slice in the sesame seeds until well coated. Reserve any leftover seeds to add to the salad at the end.

Heat a tablespoon of oil in a frying pan over a medium–low heat. Fry the sesame-crusted avocado for about 1 minute on each side, or until the sesame seeds are golden, turning them very carefully with a pair of tongs. Allow to cool.

Place the couscous in a shallow baking dish, sprinkle with sea salt, and drizzle over 1 tablespoon or so of oil. Stir to mix well. Pour the hot vegetable stock over the top and cover immediately with plastic wrap. Leave for 10 minutes. When ready, remove the plastic wrap and drizzle over another tablespoon of oil. Using a fork or chopsticks, fluff up the grains.

In a large bowl, combine the couscous, corn kernels and slices, arugula, cilantro (if using), and any leftover sesame seeds. Season well with sea salt and black pepper and drizzle over a little extra oil. To serve, transfer salad to a serving plate, top with the avocado pieces, and spoon over the lime crema to finish.

THE B.L.E.A.T

Serves 4–6

Individually, broccoli, lettuce, egg, avocado, and tomato are humble everyday ingredients. When combined, they create this smashing, crowd-pleasing salad that is surprisingly complex in flavor and texture—smoky from the charred broccoli, crunchy from the lettuce and croutons, and creamy from the avocado and tomato mayonnaise. Charred broccoli is a staple in our home. I often have a container of it ready in the fridge for a quick snack or lunch box filler.

7 ounces (200 g) stale bread, cut or
  torn into chunks
extra-virgin olive oil
1 large broccoli head
  (about 1 pound/450 g),
  cut into florets
1 head romaine lettuce, quartered
  and sliced
1 large avocado, cut into chunks
3–4 medium-boiled large eggs,
  peeled and sliced
1 tablespoon chopped chives
sea salt and black pepper

TOMATO MAYO

½ cup (125 g) good-quality mayonnaise
1 Roma tomato, finely chopped
1 tablespoon extra-virgin olive oil
1 small garlic clove, very finely chopped
2 tablespoons finely chopped chives
sea salt and black pepper

Preheat the oven to 400°F (200°C).

Place the bread chunks on a large baking sheet, drizzle over a little olive oil, and add a pinch of sea salt. Bake for 15–20 minutes, until the bread is golden and crispy.

Drizzle the broccoli with oil. Heat a grill or grill on high and, when hot, add the broccoli florets and char on all sides. Sprinkle with sea salt and set aside.

For the tomato mayo, combine the mayonnaise, tomato, oil, and garlic and stir vigorously until well mixed. Add the chives, season with a pinch of sea salt and black pepper, and stir.

In a large serving bowl, combine the broccoli, lettuce, avocado, eggs, a handful of croutons, and half the tomato mayo. Toss to combine. To serve, top with a few more spoonfuls of mayo, and another handful of croutons. Scatter over the chives, season with sea salt and black pepper, and finish with a final drizzle of extra-virgin olive oil.

TIP

Keep leftover croutons in an airtight container or resealable bag in your pantry. They are perfect for snacking on and adding crunch to your salads or soups.

For vegans, you can use vegan mayonnaise.

CACIO E PEPE BROCCOLINI WITH CRISPY WHITE BEANS

Serves 4 / gluten free

Cacio e pepe (literally "cheese and pepper") is an irresistible flavor combination. Here, I have transformed a classic pasta sauce into a minimal yet memorable salad. This dish requires only a few ingredients, the magic coming from the simple elegance of sharp cheese, freshly cracked pepper, charred broccolini, and seriously good crispy white beans. Vary the amount of black pepper to your liking, as some palates might not appreciate the excessive heat or spice.

2 bunches of broccolini
   (about 14 ounces/400 g),
   trimmed and each stem halved
extra-virgin olive oil
18 ounces (500 g) cooked cannellini or
   navy beans (about 2 drained cans)
1 garlic clove, finely chopped
handful of chopped flat-leaf
   parsley leaves
½–1 teaspoon freshly ground
   black pepper
1½ ounces (40 g) pecorino cheese,
   grated, plus extra to serve
½ lemon, cut into wedges
sea salt

Substitute

broccolini: broccoli, broccoli rabe,
cauliflower, kale

pecorino: Parmesan

Heat a large frying pan over a medium–high heat (or use a grill). Coat the broccolini stems in olive oil and fry for 2–3 minutes on each side, until there is some charring. Remove from the pan and season well with sea salt.

Place the same pan over a high heat and add a big drizzle of oil. Add the beans and fry for 2–3 minutes. Stir in the garlic, season well with sea salt, and fry for 8–10 minutes, stirring every now and then, until the beans are crispy. If the beans become dry during cooking, add more oil.

Toss the broccolini, beans, and parsley together and drizzle with a little more olive oil. Spoon onto a serving plate. Sprinkle over the black pepper and grate over the pecorino. Serve with extra pecorino and lemon wedges on the side.

PRIMAVERA RICE SALAD WITH GREMOLATA

Serves 4 / gluten free

Primavera is a dreamy depiction, referencing the lively beauty and gentility of spring. Traditionally, primavera dishes include young spring plants, such as asparagus, peas, and spring onions; often this may expand to include zucchini, bell pepper, and fava beans. This easy rice salad is a simple celebration of seasonality—it encourages you to honor fresh spring veggies, but also offers suggestions for frozen substitutes when fresh is not available. The gremolata, traditionally served with meat in Italian cuisine, adds brightness and a slight bitterness to this dish, while goat cheese injects a lovely fruitiness.

extra-virgin olive oil
2 shallots, finely diced
1 garlic clove, finely chopped
1 cup (185 g) shelled fava beans
    (or thawed frozen edamame beans)
1 cup (150 g) peas (frozen or fresh)
3 cups (450 g) cooked basmati rice
1 small fennel bulb, finely diced
1 small zucchini, finely diced
handful of basil or mint leaves or
    dill fronds (optional)
juice of 1 lemon, plus extra if needed
3½ ounces (100 g) soft goat cheese,
    crumbled
2 tablespoons sunflower seeds, toasted
sea salt and black pepper

GREMOLATA

1 garlic clove, very finely chopped
½ cup (12 g) chopped flat-leaf parsley
    leaves
3 tablespoons chopped chives
zest of 1 lemon

Substitute

basmati rice: brown rice
omit goat cheese for vegan

Heat a drizzle of olive oil in a frying pan over a medium heat, add the shallot or spring onion and the garlic, and cook for 1–2 minutes, until soft and golden. Add the fava beans and peas, season with sea salt and a turn of black pepper, and stir-fry for 1–2 minutes, until the veggies are just tender but still a little crisp.

To make the gremolata, combine the garlic with the chopped parsley and chives. Stir in the lemon zest.

Add the rice to a big bowl and toss with the fava beans, peas, fennel, zucchini, and the basil, mint, or dill, if using. Squeeze over the lemon juice and drizzle over a few big glugs of oil. Season generously with sea salt and black pepper. Taste and adjust the seasoning, oil, and citrus if necessary. Once you are happy with the seasoning, scatter over the goat cheese and sunflower seeds, and toss everything together. Serve with a sprinkle of gremolata.

TIPS

This salad is fine served without the gremolata. The gremolata can be made ahead and stored in an airtight container for 1 day.

Gremolata is also nice served on roasted veggies, pasta, and stews, and can be mixed with a little extra-virgin olive oil to make a simple herbaceous oil.

Use leftover rice for this salad.

If you are cooking rice from scratch, cook the rice in vegetable stock for more flavor.

POTATO AND CELERIAC WITH BASIL REMOULADE

Serves 4 / gluten free / vegan (use vegan mayonnaise)

I remember the heyday of celeriac remoulade; it was the 1990s and my husband—boyfriend at the time—and I were very sophisticated. We really liked fine dining. We tried truffles for the first time, and lapped up tasting menus all around Sydney. At our 1999 wedding, we served celeriac remoulade with some sort of smoked salmon. In the years since, my palate has changed considerably, but I still love celeriac remoulade. My version of this dish features roasted small potatoes and celeriac, doused in a basil-scented remoulade sauce.

1 pound (450 g) celeriac
1 pound (450 g) fingerling potatoes,
    unpeeled, cut diagonally into ½-inch
    (1.5 cm) slices
extra-virgin olive oil
1 tablespoon white wine vinegar
8 tiny cornichons or 1–2 small
    gherkins, finely chopped
2 celery stalks, finely diced
1 tablespoon chopped chives
sea salt and black pepper
3 tablespoons sunflower seeds, to serve
handful of flat-leaf parsley leaves,
    to serve (optional)

BASIL REMOULADE

¾ cup (185 g) good-quality mayonnaise
1 garlic clove, very finely chopped
¼ cup (6 g) basil leaves, finely chopped
1½ teaspoons Dijon mustard
sea salt and black pepper (optional)

Preheat the oven to 425°F (220°C).

Peel the celeriac and cut it into the same size pieces as the potatoes (be sure to work quickly, as it will brown soon after peeling). Place the celeriac and potato pieces on a baking sheet, drizzle over some olive oil, and season with sea salt and black pepper. Roast for 30–35 minutes, until golden. Remove from the oven, sprinkle with more sea salt, and immediately drizzle over the white wine vinegar. Set aside to cool.

For the remoulade, combine the mayonnaise, garlic, basil, and Dijon mustard in a bowl. Taste and season with sea salt and black pepper, if required.

In a large bowl, combine the potato, celeriac, cornichon or gherkin, celery, and chives. Add the basil remoulade and toss until everything is well coated. Taste and season with more sea salt and black pepper, if required. To serve, scatter over the sunflower seeds and parsley, if using.

TIPS

If you want to prepare the celeriac beforehand, keep it in a bowl of acidulated water (water with lemon juice) until ready to roast.

For vegans, you can use vegan mayonnaise or substitute the vegan cashew cream (see page 130) for the basil remoulade.

CABBAGE AND CARROT VERMICELLI SLAW WITH TOFU AND LEMON–POPPYSEED DRESSING

Serves 4 / gluten free / vegan (use maple syrup)

Growing up, mung bean vermicelli—or cellophane noodles—were a staple in my daily diet, included in Chinese stews, soups, and "Buddha's delight" (*lo han jai*), which my mum prepared during times of worship, such as Chinese New Year. For me, mung bean vermicelli is a sacred ingredient and every time I eat these noodles, I am reminded of home. In salads, they allow me to express my cross-cultural approach to flavor and texture.

extra-virgin olive oil
12 ounces (350 g) firm tofu,
 cut into ¼-inch (6 mm) slices
5 ounces (150 g) mung bean vermicelli,
 soaked in warm water for 15 minutes
 and drained
1 cup (100 g) shredded green cabbage
1 carrot (about 3½ ounces/100 g),
 shredded
4 scallions, finely sliced
3 tablespoons slivered almonds
sea salt and black pepper

LEMON–POPPYSEED DRESSING
juice of 1 lemon, plus extra if needed
2 tablespoons extra-virgin olive oil
1 tablespoon sesame oil
1 tablespoon honey or maple syrup,
 plus extra if needed
1 tablespoon finely chopped chives
2 teaspoons poppy seeds
1 small garlic clove, very finely chopped
sea salt and black pepper

Substitute

green cabbage: savoy cabbage,
purple cabbage, Brussels sprouts

mung bean vermicelli: rice noodles,
soba noodles

Heat a large frying pan over a medium heat. Drizzle some olive oil into the pan and add the tofu. Season the tofu well with sea salt and black pepper, and fry for 2–3 minutes on each side, until golden. Remove from the pan and set aside to cool. Slice into thin strips.

To make the dressing, whisk together the lemon juice, oils, honey or maple syrup, chives, poppy seeds, and garlic in a small bowl. Season well with sea salt and black pepper. Taste and adjust the lemon juice, olive oil, honey, and seasoning until you have a well-balanced dressing.

Bring a large pot of salted water to the boil. Add the vermicelli and cook for just 60 seconds or so, until the noodles are just translucent. Drain, refresh under cold running water, and drain again.

Place the cabbage, carrot, and scallions in a big bowl, pour over the dressing, and toss to combine. Season well with sea salt and black pepper, add the vermicelli, and toss well. To serve, drizzle with olive oil and scatter over the almonds.

SWEET-AND-SOUR CAULIFLOWER
WITH RAMEN NOODLES

Serves 4 / vegan

My mum is an ingenious cook, who is the master of using everyday pantry ingredients in very unexpected ways. As a traditional Chinese cook, you wouldn't expect that a very Western ingredient like tomato sauce would feature in her cooking. When we were growing up, my mum used tomato sauce in several unusual ways—she often added it to stir-fry dishes to add a distinct sweet and umami flavor. She also used tomato sauce to make sweet-and-sour sauce, which she served with crispy pork or tofu, often accented with canned pineapple. Here, I've teamed a classic Chinese sweet-and-sour sauce with chickpea-battered cauliflower and instant ramen noodles, in an irresistible salad to please all ages.

9 ounces (250 g) instant (or fresh) ramen noodles
1 cup (100 g) chickpea flour
1 garlic clove, very finely chopped
sunflower or vegetable oil
1 large cauliflower head (about 1¾ pounds/800 g), cut into florets
1 red bell pepper, seeded and thinly sliced
1 tablespoon sesame oil
1 tablespoon sesame seeds (white, black, or both), toasted
4 scallions, finely sliced
sea salt and white pepper

SWEET-AND-SOUR SAUCE

3 tablespoons sugar
2 tablespoons apple cider vinegar
2 tablespoons tamari or soy sauce
3 tablespoons tomato sauce
1 garlic clove, very finely chopped
1 teaspoon cornstarch

Substitute

cauliflower: broccoli, Brussels sprouts, tofu

Bring a large pot of salted water to the boil and add the ramen noodles. Cook according to the package instructions, until the noodles are just cooked. Drain and rinse under running water until the noodles are completely cold. Set aside.

In a bowl, whisk the chickpea flour, 1 cup (250 ml) of water, garlic, and a big pinch of sea salt together until smooth.

Place a frying pan over a medium–high heat and add a layer of sunflower or vegetable oil (enough to cover the bottom of the pan). When hot (test with a wooden chopstick or wooden spoon; if it sizzles, the oil is ready), dip each piece of cauliflower into the chickpea batter and carefully place it straight into the oil. Fry for 1–2 minutes on each side, until golden all over. Remove and place on absorbent paper towel. Sprinkle with sea salt. Repeat this process until you have fried all the cauliflower, making sure you are controlling the temperature of the oil at all times—increasing and reducing the heat as needed—to ensure that you get an even, golden color.

To make the sweet-and-sour sauce, add the sugar, vinegar, tamari or soy sauce, tomato sauce, and garlic to a small saucepan and place over a low heat. Stir and bring to the boil. Whisk the cornstarch together with 2 tablespoons of cold water until dissolved, then slowly stir the cornstarch mixture into the pan, reduce the heat to low, and continue stirring for 1–2 minutes, until the sauce is thickened.

Combine the cauliflower with the sweet-and-sour sauce. Toss together well.

Combine the noodles with the red bell pepper slices and sesame oil, season with sea salt and white pepper, and toss together. To serve, top the noodles with the sweet and sour cauliflower and scatter over the sesame seeds and the scallions.

ROASTED DELICATA SQUASH
WITH CHICKPEAS AND TURMERIC TAHINI

Serves 4 / gluten free / vegan

I thank my dear friend Jodi Moreno for introducing me to the wonderful world of delicata squash. The first time I tried it, Jodi had brought a plate of delicata, smothered in tahini, for an autumn potluck dinner. From that day on, delicata and I have been inseparable. Delicata squash signify the arrival of autumn in New York, as their signature stripy skin and long oval shape proliferate around farmers' markets. Rich in flavor, with a mellow brown sugar taste, delicata boast a thin skin that is tender enough to be roasted and eaten—no peeling required. I bulk up the sweetness in this salad with the wizardry of maple syrup and balance it all with an earthy, nutty tahini sauce.

3 delicata squash
    (about 3½-4½ pounds/1.5–2 kg)
2 teaspoons cumin seeds
extra-virgin olive oil
1 tablespoon maple syrup
7 ounces (200 g) cooked chickpeas
    (about ¾ drained can)
handful of baby arugula or
    spinach leaves
handful of cilantro leaves (optional)
2 handfuls of microgreens (any variety)
sea salt and black pepper

TURMERIC TAHINI
⅓ cup (90 g) tahini
1½ teaspoons ground turmeric
juice of ½ small lemon
1 tablespoon maple syrup
2 tablespoons extra-virgin olive oil
sea salt and black pepper

Substitute

delicata: butternut squash,
kabocha pumpkin or sweet potato

chickpeas: cannellini or borlotti beans

maple syrup: honey

Preheat the oven to 400˚ F (200˚C).

Slice the delicata squash, with the skin on, into ½-inch (1 cm) thick rounds. Scoop out the seeds and discard. Place the delicata slices on a large baking sheet and sprinkle over the cumin seeds. Drizzle with olive oil, season with sea salt, and toss to coat. Roast for 20–25 minutes, until tender and turning golden. Remove from the oven and drizzle with the maple syrup. Set aside to cool.

To make the turmeric tahini, whisk the tahini, turmeric, lemon juice, maple syrup, and olive oil together with about 3 tablespoons of water until smooth. You may need to adjust the amount of lemon juice, oil, and water to achieve the right flavor balance and consistency for your taste. Season well with sea salt and black pepper.

In a large bowl, combine the delicata with the chickpeas, arugula, and cilantro, if using. Add a few spoonfuls of the turmeric tahini and fold it through the salad. To serve, transfer to a serving plate, season with sea salt and black pepper, drizzle with extra-virgin olive oil, and scatter over the microgreens to finish.

TIP
This tahini dressing can be made ahead and kept in an airtight container in the fridge for up to 7 days.

MASSAGED KALE WITH QUINOA, RICOTTA, AND CRISPY SHIITAKE

Serves 4

Massaging kale tenderizes it and breaks down some of the bitterness. But massaging kale with tomato and garlic takes it on a whole new exciting journey. With these flavorful leaves as your base, throw in some quinoa for heartiness, ricotta for creaminess, and crispy shiitakes for crunch. These shiitake chips will blow your mind and may sway even mushroom-phobics to embrace fungus. I could snack on these all day.

1 cup (200 g) quinoa, rinsed
2 cups (500 ml) vegetable stock
1 large tomato, finely diced
1 garlic clove, very finely chopped
extra-virgin olive oil
1 bunch of kale, stems removed and leaves torn
1 tablespoon chopped chives
¾ cup (180 g) whole-milk ricotta
sea salt and black pepper

SHIITAKE CHIPS

14 ounces (400 g) fresh shiitake mushrooms, stems removed, sliced
2 tablespoons tamari
2 tablespoons apple cider vinegar
2 tablespoons maple syrup
½ teaspoon smoked paprika
1–2 tablespoons extra-virgin olive oil

Preheat the oven to 350° F (180° C). Line a baking sheet with parchment paper.

To make the shiitake chips, place the shiitake slices in a small bowl. Combine the tamari, vinegar, maple syrup, smoked paprika, and oil, add to the mushrooms, and mix well to coat. Lay out the mushrooms on the prepared baking sheet and roast for 40 minutes, stirring halfway through, until the mushrooms are shrivelled and crispy. Remove and set aside.

Place the quinoa in a saucepan, pour over the vegetable stock, and bring to the boil. Reduce the heat to low, cover, and leave to simmer for about 15–20 minutes. Once the water has been absorbed, turn off the heat, uncover, and allow to sit for 5–10 minutes. Fluff up with a fork.

Combine the tomato and garlic and season with a big pinch of sea salt and a drizzle of oil. Massage this mixture into the kale leaves in a large bowl. Allow to sit for 10 minutes.

Add the quinoa and chives to the kale. Add the ricotta and toss to combine. Drizzle with olive oil and season with sea salt and black pepper. To serve, transfer salad to a serving plate and scatter the shiitake chips over the top.

TIPS

To get ahead, you can prepare the shiitake mushrooms the day before and leave them to marinate overnight in the fridge before roasting. This also allows the flavors to develop.

Shiitake chips can be stored in an airtight container in the pantry for up to 7 days.

SUSHI SALAD

Serves 4 / gluten free / vegan

Brown rice bowls have become a midweek staple in our home. Extremely adaptable, they allow me to use up whatever vegetables are in my fridge and are a great way to enjoy leftover roasted vegetables. I had originally named this dish "Miso Brown Rice Salad with Avocado, Edamame, and Seaweed," but my kids proclaimed it the "Sushi Salad" when I brought it to the table, so hence it is named. For extra protein, try topping the salad with a fried or hard-boiled egg.

2 cups (300 g) frozen shelled edamame beans
4 cups (740 g) cooked brown rice
4 Persian cucumbers, sliced into rounds
3 avocados, peeled and sliced
2 handfuls of baby spinach leaves
extra-virgin olive oil
1 tablespoon sesame seeds (white, black, or both), toasted
4 nori seaweed sheets, toasted and cut into thin strips
sea salt and black pepper

SESAME–MISO DRESSING
3 tablespoons miso paste
1 tablespoon toasted sesame oil
1 tablespoon mirin
1 teaspoon sugar
1 teaspoon sesame seeds (white, black, or both), toasted

Bring a small pot of salted water to the boil and add the edamame. Cook for 1–2 minutes, until they are tender yet still crunchy. Drain and run under cold water.

To make the dressing, whisk together the miso paste, sesame oil, mirin, sugar, and 1–2 tablespoons of water until well combined—you want the consistency of cream. Stir in the sesame seeds.

In a large bowl, combine the rice, edamame, cucumber, avocado, and baby spinach and toss together gently. To serve, transfer salad to a serving plate, drizzle over the sesame–miso dressing and a little olive oil, season with sea salt and black pepper, and top with the sesame seeds and nori strips.

TOFU LARB WITH
QUICK-PICKLED ONIONS IN LETTUCE CUPS

Serves 4 / gluten free / vegan

Larb is a traditional meat-based salad from Laos and Thailand, where stir-fried ground meat is flavored with a zesty umami sauce made with fish sauce, chiles, and herbs. My vegan version is a mash-up of larb and Chinese *sang choy bau*, with pan-fried tofu, quick-pickled red onion, and a bright lime dressing all enveloped in a lettuce cup. If you prefer, serve your larb with rice.

1 tablespoon sunflower or olive oil

2 garlic cloves, very finely chopped

2 shallots, finely diced

1 lemongrass stalk, white part only, finely chopped

1¾ pounds (800 g) extra-firm tofu, crumbled

2 kaffir lime leaves, very finely sliced (optional, but recommended)

handful of mint, cilantro, or Thai basil leaves

20 iceberg or butter lettuce leaves

1 lime, halved

½ cup (20 g) crispy fried onions (store-bought)

sea salt

QUICK-PICKLED ONIONS

½ cup (125 ml) apple cider vinegar

1 tablespoon sugar

1 teaspoon sea salt

1 small red onion, thinly shaved or sliced

LIME DRESSING

3 tablespoons lime juice

1 tablespoon rice vinegar

2 tablespoons brown sugar

1 red chile, seeded and finely chopped (use less or more to your taste)

Substitute

tofu: mushrooms

For the quick-pickled onions, whisk together the vinegar, sugar, and salt with ½ cup (125 ml) of water. Place the onion in a jar and pour the vinegar mixture over. Leave to sit at room temperature for 20–60 minutes.

Make the lime dressing by whisking all the ingredients together in a small bowl.

Add the oil to a wok or large frying pan over a high heat. Toss in the garlic, shallot, and lemongrass and cook for 60 seconds. Add the tofu and toss for 2–3 minutes, until the tofu is heated through and golden. Remove from the heat and transfer to a bowl. Leave to cool for 1 minute, then fold through the lime dressing, kaffir lime leaves, if using, and herbs. Season with sea salt.

To serve, place a big spoonful of the tofu mixture into a lettuce leaf cup. Top with a few pickled onions, and a squeeze of lime, and then scatter with crispy onions. Fold it all up and pop it straight into your mouth!

TIP

The dressing can be made in advance and kept in the fridge for up to 1 week.

Kaffir leaves are often used in Thai and Southesast Asian cooking. They add an aromatic, floral brightness to curries, stir-fries, and soups. Find fresh or frozen kaffir lime leaves at Thai supermarkets—don't be tempted to use the dried leaves in salads (though they are fine in curries) as only the fresh ones are eaten raw. If you can't find them, that's fine—just omit.

ORANGE, FENNEL, AND OLIVE SALAD

Serves 2 as a main or 4 as a side / gluten free / vegan

This is the simplest of salads, featuring the very classic Italian triumvirate of orange, fennel, and salty olive. This salad is an unlikely favorite at our family table. Discovering that my kids enjoy raw fennel has been a huge revelation for me—now they eat fennel as a crudité, in their lunch boxes, and in many salads. In this dish, the subtle aniseed tones of the fennel are perfectly offset by the sweet, juicy orange and salty olive. The apple cider dressing adds a sweet touch—but if you are short on time, you can skip it altogether and just finish the dish with a copious drizzle of olive oil and a liberal seasoning of sea salt and black pepper. This is an easy dish to serve on the side with a bake, or as a part of a salad smorgasbord.

2 sweet oranges
1 large fennel bulb, very thinly shaved
or sliced, fronds reserved
⅓ cup (60 g) wrinkly black olives, pitted
handful of flat-leaf parsley and basil
leaves, torn
extra-virgin olive oil
sea salt and black pepper

APPLE CIDER DRESSING

1 small garlic clove, very finely chopped
1 tablespoon apple cider vinegar,
plus extra if needed
2 tablespoons extra-virgin olive oil,
plus extra if needed
sea salt and black pepper

Cut the top and bottom off the first orange and stand it up on a cutting board. Using a sharp paring knife and working from the top down, cut away the peel and as much of the white pith as you can. Now, hold the orange in the palm of your hand—have a bowl ready to catch 1–2 tablespoons of the juice for the dressing—and cut between the membranes to segment the orange. Repeat with the second orange.

Prepare the dressing by whisking together all the ingredients. Taste and adjust the oil, vinegar, and seasoning if necessary, adding the reserved orange juice if you like, until you achieve your preferred balance.

Combine the orange segments with the shaved fennel, olives, parsley, and basil. Pour over the dressing, drizzle with olive oil, and finish with a final sprinkle of sea salt, lots of black pepper, and a scattering of fennel fronds.

WALDORF-ESQUE SALAD WITH ROASTED BALSAMIC GRAPES, BURRATA, AND CANDIED PECANS

Serves 4 / gluten free

The Waldorf salad has stood the test of time. First created in 1896, at the Waldorf Hotel in New York City, it appeared in a cookbook for the first time in 1928; ninety years later, here is another incarnation of this salad. Through the years, the salad has remained faithful to its origins—the original version contained only apples, celery, and mayonnaise; later, walnuts became an integral part of the dish. My take on this classic is not traditional, but it is Waldorf-esque in finish. Balsamic-roasted grapes provide a subtle sweetness, while the kale is a modern, earthy touch. Yogurt lightens up the salad from its usual mayonnaise base, but the luxury is added via a ball of torn burrata and addictive candied pecans.

½ bunch of kale, stems removed
   and leaves torn
extra-virgin olive oil
9 ounces (250 g) red seedless grapes
2 tablespoons white balsamic vinegar
2 thyme sprigs, leaves picked
½ cup (125 g) Greek yogurt
juice of ½ lemon
1 large red apple (such as Red Delicious
   or Fuji), cored and thinly sliced
1 celery stalk, finely chopped
1 burrata or mozzarella ball
   (about 8 ounces/225 g), torn into
   large chunks
sea salt and black pepper

CANDIED PECANS

1 large egg white, beaten
1 tablespoon maple syrup
¼ teaspoon ground cinnamon
½ teaspoon sea salt, plus extra
   for sprinkling
1 cup (125 g) pecans

Substitute

kale: spinach, arugula
red grapes: green grapes

Preheat the oven to 375°F (190°C).

Place the kale in a large bowl, drizzle with some olive oil, and sprinkle with sea salt. Massage the kale to soften the leaves. Leave to sit for 10 minutes.

Place the grapes on a baking sheet, drizzle over some oil and the white balsamic, season with sea salt, and sprinkle over the thyme leaves. Toss to coat the grapes. Roast for 10 minutes, until the grapes are starting to burst. Remove from the oven and set aside.

Reduce the oven temperature to 300°F (150°C) and line a baking sheet with parchment paper.

To make the candied pecans, combine the egg white, maple syrup, cinnamon, and sea salt in a medium bowl. Add the pecans and toss to coat well. Lay the pecans out on the prepared baking sheet in a single layer and bake in the oven for 40 minutes, turning every 15 minutes, until the nuts are golden. Remove from the oven and sprinkle with sea salt.

Combine the yogurt and lemon juice. Place the kale, apple, and celery in a large bowl and add the yogurt mixture, along with a generous drizzle of olive oil and a pinch of sea salt. Toss everything together.

To serve, arrange the kale and apple mixture on a serving platter, top with the roasted grapes and all their pan juices, dot with the burrata or mozzarella, and scatter over the candied pecans. Finish with a final drizzle of olive oil and another pinch of sea salt and black pepper.

CANTALOUPE, HALLOUMI, AND QUICK-PICKLED SHALLOT SALAD

Serves 4, as a light dish / gluten free

Fruit in a savory salad is an acquired taste. It took me many years to come around to this particular delicacy. However, when we moved to America, my palate became more open to the savory "fruit salads," which are ubiquitous here during the summer. I've seen strawberry with soba noodles (a genius invention by food stylist and general legend Susan Spungen—Google it!), mango with spicy carrots, grapefruit with fennel and avocado, peach with cucumber, and peach-based caprese salads. Fruit is the real salad deal here. For me, the key was discovering that certain fruits like melons, peaches, apples, and grapes pair very well with cheese. I originally made this recipe with watermelon, which gave a juicier finish. Cantaloupe is a little more controlled in texture, and teams perfectly with the salty Halloumi cheese, peppery arugula, pickled shallots, and bright basil.

9 ounces (250 g) Halloumi cheese,
    cut into ½-inch (1 cm) slices
extra-virgin olive oil
4 handfuls of baby arugula leaves
11 ounces (300 g) cantaloupe, cut into
    ¾-inch (2 cm) cubes
handful of basil leaves, roughly torn
juice of ½ lime
sea salt and black pepper

QUICK-PICKLED SHALLOTS

1 shallot, very finely sliced
1 tablespoon apple cider vinegar
½ teaspoon sugar
pinch of coriander seeds
pinch of sea salt

Substitute

cantaloupe: watermelon, peaches

To make the quick-pickled shallots, place the shallot slices in a small bowl and pour over the apple cider vinegar. Toss to combine, then add the rest of the ingredients together with 1 tablespoon of water. Toss again. Allow the shallot to pickle for at least 10 minutes.

Heat a grill, grill pan, or frying pan until hot. Coat the Halloumi slices in a few small glugs of oil and gently cook for 1–2 minutes on each side, until golden.

Arrange the arugula leaves over a large platter. Scatter over the cantaloupe cubes and torn basil. Tear the Halloumi slices in half and add them, along with some drained pickled shallots, to the salad. Squeeze over the lime juice, drizzle over some olive oil, and season with sea salt and black pepper. Serve immediately.

TIPS

The quick-pickled shallots can be made a day ahead and allowed to pickle in the fridge overnight.

Leftover pickled shallots can be stored in an airtight jar and kept in the fridge for up to 4 weeks.

GRILLED PEACH SALAD WITH MOZZARELLA, BASIL, AND HONEY

Serves 4, as a light dish / gluten free

During the summer, grilled peaches are a surprisingly pleasant main meal ingredient. Use them in caprese salads, as a pizza topping, or pickle them. Reserve this salad for when peaches are at their most abundant and sweet, and choose peaches that are on the firm side, as they will soften up and sweeten with cooking. This is a perfectly light, slightly creamy, and subtly earthy dish for warm evenings.

6 yellow or white peaches
extra-virgin olive oil
2 handfuls of mixed salad leaves
1 pound (450 g) fresh mozzarella
handful of basil leaves, torn
sea salt and black pepper
1–2 tablespoons honey

Cut each peach in half, remove the pit, and then slice each half into four thick wedges. Place the peach wedges in a large bowl and drizzle over some olive oil.

Heat a grill or grill pan until searing hot, then add the peach wedges and grill for a minute or so on each cut side, until there are char marks and the flesh is starting to soften. (Don't cook for too long, as you don't want mushy peaches—you still want the flesh to retain some firmness.)

Arrange the salad leaves on a large platter and scatter over the peach wedges. Tear up the mozzarella, dot it amongst the peaches, and top with the basil leaves. To serve, drizzle generously with olive oil, season with sea salt and black pepper, and trickle over the honey.

SOUPY
SALADS

SOUPS ARE HEALTH.

At my childhood table, soup was an elixir, a daily ritual to bring good health. Before bone broths became a luxury item, there was my mum's nightly medicinal broth, a meal disguised as a soup, brimming with potent Chinese medicinal herbs, promising healing powers and the balancing of yin (cool) and yang (heat). My soupy salads are inspired by my mum's inclusive soups—they are complete meals of epic proportions. These recipes are rich in plentiful ingredients and flavor, constructed with the attitude of a full-bodied salad, but transformed into a nutritious, robust, healing soup.

LENTIL SOUP WITH
FETA-ROASTED CAULIFLOWER AND WALNUTS

Serves 6 / gluten free

I recently wrote a story about comfort food and, during my research, one dish was consistently cited as a favorite comforting dish—lentil soup. Indeed, this humble soup is a mainstay across several diverse cultures, a popular dish in Greek, Israeli, Middle Eastern, and Southeast Asian families. For me, this soup represents "pantry cooking" at its best, as I always have the bones of this recipe—lentils, carrot, celery, onion, tomato paste—in my larder. The feta-roasted cauliflower with walnuts is optional, but highly recommended.

extra-virgin olive oil
1 large carrot, finely diced
1 small yellow onion, diced
2 celery stalks, finely diced
1 garlic clove, finely chopped
4 ounces (110 g) tomato paste
2 cups (400 g) green lentils, rinsed
2 bay leaves
8 cups (2 liters) vegetable stock
2 tablespoons red wine vinegar
sea salt and black pepper

FETA-ROASTED CAULIFLOWER
WITH WALNUTS
½ cauliflower head
    (about 14 ounces/400 g),
    chopped into bite-sized pieces
extra-virgin olive oil
½ teaspoon dried oregano
small pinch of red chile flakes
1 cup (140 g) feta, crumbled
½ cup (70 g) walnuts, roughly chopped
handful of flat-leaf parsley leaves,
    roughly chopped
sea salt and black pepper

Substitute

tomato paste: 2 fresh tomatoes, diced
green lentils: brown, black, or Puy lentils
omit feta for vegan

Preheat the oven to 425°F (220°C).

For the feta-roasted cauliflower, place the cauliflower on a baking sheet, coat with a drizzle of olive oil, and season with sea salt and black pepper. Add the oregano, chile flakes, and feta and toss to combine. Roast for 10 minutes, then remove the tray from the oven, add the walnuts, and toss everything together. Roast for a further 7–8 minutes, until the cauliflower is golden and the walnuts are crispy. Remove from the oven and allow to cool for a few minutes. Add the parsley and toss to combine.

Place a Dutch oven or saucepan over a medium heat. Drizzle with olive oil and add the carrot, onion, and celery. Cook for 5 minutes, until starting to soften. Add the garlic and cook for another 2 minutes, until the vegetables are slightly caramelized. Finally, stir the tomato paste through the vegetables and fry for another 2 minutes.

Add the lentils, bay leaves, and stock to the vegetable and tomato mixture. Cover and simmer over a low heat for about 20 minutes, until the lentils are soft. Finish with the red wine vinegar and season well with sea salt and black pepper. To serve, ladle into bowls and add a big spoonful of the roasted cauliflower.

TIP

This soup can be consumed immediately, or stored in the fridge overnight for even deeper flavors.

BLACK BEAN SOUP WITH CHIPOTLE TORTILLA CHIPS

Serves 4–6 / gluten free / vegan

Black bean soup is an all-American classic—boldly flavored, deeply nurturing, and deliciously wholesome. It is a vegetarian dish that never fails to impress around our table. Beans can be bland, so as a general rule, whether in soups or salads, season them generously with both salt and spice. I use canned beans and all their brine here—this is the trick to achieving a thick soup in a short amount of time. If you have two hours to spare, please use dried black beans (you don't need to soak them). I don't bother puréeing the soup as I prefer the texture of some whole beans. Instead, take a potato masher and stab the soup a few times just to break up some of the beans and release starch into the soup to thicken it up (without turning it into black sludge).

extra-virgin olive oil
1 yellow onion, finely diced
3 thyme sprigs
2 garlic cloves, finely chopped
2 bay leaves
1 tablespoon ground cumin
2 teaspoons ground coriander
½ teaspoon smoked paprika
1 green bell pepper, seeded and
    finely diced
15 ounces (425 g) tomato passata
    or purée
27 ounces (750 g) cooked black beans
    (about 3 cans)
3 cups (750 ml) vegetable stock
½ cup (65 g) pumpkin seeds, toasted
handful of cilantro leaves
sea salt and black pepper

CHIPOTLE TORTILLA CHIPS

4 corn tortillas
extra-virgin olive oil
small pinch of chipotle powder
sea salt

Preheat the oven to 400°F (200°C).

For the chipotle tortilla chips, brush each side of the corn tortillas with olive oil and stack them on top of each other. Cut them in half, then slice each half into ¼-inch (6 mm) strips. Spread the tortilla strips out in a single layer on a large baking sheet, sprinkle over the chipotle powder and salt, and toss gently. Bake for 10–15 minutes, until crispy.

In a large pan over a medium–high heat, drizzle some olive oil and add the onion and thyme. Cook for 2 minutes, stirring, then toss in the garlic and bay leaves. Add the cumin, coriander, and smoked paprika and cook for 1 minute. Add the bell pepper, tomato passata, black beans with brine, and vegetable stock, reduce the heat to medium, and cook for 15 minutes.

Remove the bay leaves and thyme sprigs. Taste the soup and season with sea salt and black pepper. Using a potato masher or the back of a large fork, randomly mash up some of the beans. This will thicken up the soup and create a lovely texture.

Ladle the soup into bowls and serve topped with the tortilla chips, pumpkin seeds, and cilantro leaves.

SWEET CORN EGG DROP NOODLE SOUP

Serves 4 / gluten free

As kids, creamed corn, usually from a can, was a quick and satisfying snack for us. My mother would make wonderful things with a can of creamed corn—steamed egg custards, toasties, stews and, my favorite, a simple but amazing corn egg drop soup. Here, I've added a little mung bean vermicelli to take this soup to main meal status.

1 tablespoon extra-virgin olive oil

1-inch (2.5 cm) piece of ginger, peeled and finely chopped

1 large garlic clove, finely chopped

6 cups (1.5 liters) vegetable stock

4 cups (800 g) sweet corn kernels (fresh or frozen)

1 tablespoon potato starch, mixed with 2 tablespoons of water

1½ ounces (40 g) mung bean vermicelli, soaked in warm water for 15 minutes

2 large eggs, lightly beaten

3 tablespoons sesame seeds, toasted

handful of chopped chives

sesame oil, to drizzle

sea salt and white pepper

Substitute

mung bean vermicelli: rice vermicelli, orzo pasta

Add the olive oil to a large saucepan and place over a medium heat. Once hot, add the ginger and garlic and cook for 30 seconds, then add the stock and three-quarters of the sweet corn kernels and bring to the boil. Once boiling, reduce the heat to medium–low and, while stirring the soup, add the potato starch mixture. Cook for 5 minutes, until the soup has thickened slightly.

Drain the mung bean vermicelli and add to the soup. The noodles will cook in about 30 seconds—they will become completely transparent. Season well with sea salt and a pinch of white pepper. Slowly pour in the beaten egg, stirring clockwise constantly to create long strands of egg.

Ladle the soup into serving bowls and top with sesame seeds, chives, the remaining sweet corn, and a drizzle of sesame oil.

TIPS

The mung bean vermicelli will continue to expand and absorb the soup if it is allowed to sit. To avoid a bowl of noodles (rather than soup), add the noodles just before serving and eat immediately.

You can also make the soup ahead of time and just add the dropped egg and vermicelli when ready to eat.

ROASTED CHESTNUT AND CREMINI MUSHROOM SOUP

Serves 4–6 / gluten free / vegan

This is my Thanksgiving soup. It's a bowlful of contrasts—delicate yet rich, earthy yet creamy, airy yet densely flavored—the perfect show-stopping soup to serve alongside a hearty, celebratory meal. Chestnuts are wintry and warming, and always remind me of my first trip to Europe as an eighteen-year-old, where chestnuts roasted on the beautiful streets of London, Paris, and Rome. If you have the time, and are so inclined, roast your own chestnuts for this soup—the flavor will be even richer. But pre-roasted, store-bought chestnuts are a fantastic pantry resource, and allow you to enjoy this celebration soup any day of the week.

extra-virgin olive oil
1 yellow onion, finely diced
1 garlic clove, chopped
6 thyme sprigs
9 ounces (250 g) cremini mushrooms, thinly sliced
18 ounces (500 g) roasted chestnuts
8 cups (2 liters) vegetable stock
1 cup (150 g) cashews, soaked in boiling water for 30 minutes then drained
3 tablespoons chopped chives
sea salt and black pepper

Substitute

pre-roasted chestnuts: fresh chestnuts to roast

cremini mushrooms: wild mushrooms, button mushrooms

cashews: almonds

Add the olive oil to a large pot and place over a medium heat. When hot, add the onion and cook for 1 minute to soften slightly. Toss in the garlic, thyme, and mushrooms and sauté for 5 minutes, allowing the mushrooms to soften. Stir in the chestnuts and cook for a further 5–7 minutes, until everything is golden.

Setting aside about ½ cup of the mushroom and chestnut mixture to garnish the soup, add the stock and the cashews to the pot, cover, and simmer for 30 minutes, until the chestnuts are falling apart. Taste and season with sea salt and black pepper. Remove the pot from the heat and, using a hand-held blender or food processor, blitz the soup until very smooth. If the soup is too thick, add some water to loosen it up.

To serve, ladle the soup into individual bowls, top with the reserved golden chestnuts and mushrooms, scatter over the chives, and finish with a drizzle of olive oil.

TOMATO AND CANNELLINI BEAN SOUP
WITH PARMESAN KALE CHIPS

Serves 4–6 / gluten free

The moral of this recipe is that you should always keep cans of tomatoes and white beans in your pantry. Because when you do, you can whip up this flavor-bursting soup with very minimal effort. My family adores tomato soup—we usually eat it with cheese toasties (grilled cheese) for dipping! This tomato soup really has deep, complex notes—the secret is in caramelizing the whole peeled tomatoes, which adds a smoky element. Any white beans will work in this recipe. You can also use freshly cooked cannellini beans if you wish. As is often the case, this soup tastes better once it has had time to sit. Make in the morning, eat at night. Or better yet, enjoy it the next day for even deeper flavors.

extra-virgin olive oil
1 large can (1¾ pounds/800 g) whole
 peeled tomatoes, tomatoes removed
 and liquid reserved
1 yellow onion, diced
1 fennel bulb, finely diced,
 fronds reserved
2 garlic cloves, finely chopped
¼–½ teaspoon red chile flakes
1 tablespoon sherry vinegar
18 ounces (500 g) cooked cannellini
 beans (about 2 drained cans)
4 cups (1 liter) vegetable stock
sea salt and black pepper

PARMESAN KALE CHIPS

1 bunch of kale, stems removed
 and leaves torn
extra-virgin olive oil
½ cup (40 g) grated Parmesan
sea salt

Substitute

cannellini beans: butter beans,
navy beans, red kidney beans

fennel: celery

omit kale chips for vegan

Preheat the oven to 275˚F (140˚C).

For the Parmesan kale chips, wash and thoroughly dry the kale leaves. Place them on a large baking sheet, drizzle with a little olive oil, and sprinkle over the Parmesan. Massage the oil and cheese into the leaves, then place in the oven and roast for 20–25 minutes, until the leaves are crispy. Remove from the oven and sprinkle with sea salt. Set aside.

Place a Dutch oven or pot over a medium–high heat and add a big drizzle of olive oil. Add the tomatoes and a good pinch of sea salt and leave to cook, undisturbed, for about 4–6 minutes, until the tomatoes are caramelized and slightly charred on one side. Transfer the tomatoes and all their juices to a plate and set aside.

In the same pot, add another big drizzle of olive oil, then add the onion, fennel, garlic, and red chile flakes. Cook, stirring, until the vegetables are soft and starting to caramelize. Stir in the vinegar, caramelized tomatoes, reserved tomato liquid, drained beans, and vegetable stock, bring to a simmer, and season with sea salt and black pepper. Cover and cook for 30–40 minutes, until the flavors have melded. Use the back of a wooden spoon to break up the tomatoes.

Serve bowls of soup topped with the kale chips and a few fennel fronds.

TIPS

This soup can be made ahead and stored in the fridge for up to 2 days.

Double the Parmesan kale chips recipe and keep them for snacks. Store them in an airtight container in the pantry for 5–7 days. They are delicious!

CREAMY BROCCOLI SOUP
WITH CHEESY MACARONI

Serves 4

Broccoli is my favorite vegetable and it is the one I turn to constantly for a hearty, comforting, yet healthy meal. This is my take on the classic "cream of broccoli" soup, but without the cream! Instead, I use tofu to deliver a rich yet undeniably delicate creaminess to this soup. The lightness of the soup is unashamedly counterbalanced by the cheeky mac and cheese topping, adding an indulgent edge to this otherwise virtuous dish. Use whichever small pasta you have in your pantry for the cheesy pasta, and for vegans, you can omit the pasta altogether, or simply dress it in olive oil and salt for a dish that is equally delicious.

extra-virgin olive oil
1 yellow onion, diced
2 garlic cloves, chopped
1 teaspoon fennel seeds
2 small broccoli heads
   (about 1 ¾ pounds/750 g),
   cut into florets and stems trimmed
   and roughly chopped
5 cups (1.25 liters) vegetable stock
12 ounces (340 g) silken tofu, crumbled
handful of basil leaves, sliced
sea salt and black pepper

CHEESY MACARONI

5 ounces (150 g) macaroni
2 ounces (50 g) mascarpone
½ cup (60 g) grated cheddar
sea salt and black pepper

Heat a drizzle of olive oil in a Dutch oven or saucepan over a medium heat. Add the onion, garlic, and fennel seeds and cook for 3–4 minutes, until softened. Add the broccoli florets and stems and cook for 5 minutes, to char the broccoli slightly. Add the stock and bring to the boil, then reduce the heat to a gentle simmer and cook for 5–7 minutes, until the broccoli is tender. Stir in the tofu and season with sea salt and black pepper.

Meanwhile, for the cheesy macaroni, bring a pot of salted water to the boil and add the pasta. Cook according to the package instructions until the pasta is soft. Drain, reserving about 3 tablespoons of cooking liquid. Return the drained pasta to the same pot together with a drizzle of oil and add the reserved cooking water, mascarpone, and cheddar. Stir to melt the cheese and season with sea salt and black pepper.

Using a hand-held blender or food processor, blitz the broccoli soup until it is very smooth.

Ladle the soup into bowls and top with spoonfuls of the cheesy macaroni. Scatter with the basil and finish with a drizzle of olive oil.

TURMERIC CHICKPEA SOUP
WITH CHARRED BRUSSELS SPROUTS

Serves 4 / gluten free / vegan

Turmeric is a spice that has worked its way more and more onto my plate, and into my heart. It's a big flavor, with a smokiness and pungency that is hard to quell. When I use turmeric, I go all in. I commit to the big flavor and counterbalance it with a hint of sweetness, just like in the delicata squash and turmeric tahini salad on page 63. In this soup, the sweetness of falling apart chickpeas and coconut milk balances beautifully with the earthy aromatics of turmeric. Top it all off with the mustard notes of charred Brussels sprouts and a generous handful of scallions and cilantro, if you like.

1½ cups (300 g) dried chickpeas or 27 ounces (750 g) cooked chickpeas (about 3 drained cans), rinsed
extra-virgin olive oil
1 large yellow onion, diced
2 garlic cloves, roughly chopped
1½ teaspoons ground turmeric (or 2 tablespoons freshly grated turmeric root)
1 thyme sprig
4 cups (1 liter) vegetable stock
1⅔ cups (400 ml) coconut milk (1 can)
9 ounces (250 g) Brussels sprouts, each cut into 6 wedges
big handful of chopped scallions and cilantro leaves (optional)
2 tablespoons pumpkin seeds, toasted
sea salt and black pepper

Substitute

Brussels sprouts: broccoli rabe, broccoli, cauliflower

If you are using dried chickpeas, place them in a bowl and add enough cold water to cover by 2 inches (5 cm). Leave them to soak overnight, then drain when ready to use.

Add a drizzle of olive oil to a large pot over a medium heat. Add the onion, garlic, turmeric, thyme, and a pinch of salt and cook for 3–4 minutes, until the onion is soft. Add the chickpeas, along with the vegetable stock, and bring to the boil. Reduce the heat, cover and simmer for 1½–2 hours, until the chickpeas are very soft and falling apart—if you are using canned chickpeas, simmer for 30 minutes only. Discard the thyme sprig and stir in the coconut milk.

While the chickpeas are cooking, make the charred Brussels sprouts. Heat a frying pan over a high heat, add a big drizzle of olive oil, and add the Brussels sprouts to the pan. Season with sea salt and black pepper and cook for 2–3 minutes on each side, until the sprouts are charred and slightly crispy all over. Set aside.

Using a hand-held blender or food processor, purée the soup, working in batches if necessary and adding a few tablespoons of water if too thick, until the soup is smooth and silky. Season well with sea salt.

To serve, ladle the soup into serving bowls and top with the charred Brussels sprouts, scallions, and cilantro, if using. Sprinkle each bowl with pumpkin seeds.

TIP

This soup can be made ahead and stored in an airtight container in the fridge—without the Brussels sprouts and herbs—for 2 days. It can also be frozen for up to 3 months.

LEMON AND PEARL BARLEY SOUP

Serves 4–6 / vegan

I have always loved using lemon to add brightness to my salads, but lately I have embraced lemons more as the leading flavor of a dish. This lemon soup is inspired by a citrusy Greek chicken broth called avgolemono— my version features pearl barley and chickpeas for maximum heartiness. A simple, vibrant soup for days when you need extra comfort.

1 yellow onion, finely diced
extra-virgin olive oil
1 garlic clove, finely chopped
3 thyme sprigs, leaves picked
1 cup (220 g) pearl barley
8 cups (2 liters) vegetable stock
9 ounces (250 g) cooked chickpeas
    (about 1 drained can)
juice of ½–1 lemon, plus extra
    wedges to serve
handful of chopped flat-leaf
    parsley leaves
sea salt and black pepper

Substitute

pearl barley: pearl (Israeli) couscous or
rice (for gluten free)

Place a large pot over a medium–low heat and add the onion, along with a good drizzle of olive oil. Cook for 2 minutes until the onion has softened, then add the garlic and thyme leaves. Cook for another 2–3 minutes on low heat, stirring, until the onion is translucent but not colored.

Add the pearl barley and stock to the pan. Cook for 40–45 minutes, until the pearl barley is completely soft and starting to break down. Stir in the chickpeas, along with the lemon juice, adjusting the level of citrus to suit your individual taste—I love it very lemony. Cook until everything is heated through. Season with sea salt and lots of black pepper.

To serve, ladle the soup into bowls and finish with a drizzle of olive oil, a scattering of parsley, and extra lemon wedges on the side.

ROASTED GARLIC AND POTATO SOUP
WITH FRIED ALMONDS

Serves 4–6 / gluten free

This soup is a celebration of ordinary ingredients—garlic, potatoes, almonds—and their transformation into a spectacular family meal. Roasted, caramelized garlic is sweet and intoxicating, and is easier for the body to digest. Eat roasted cloves straight up, add them to pasta, or mash with sour cream for a full-flavored dip. Added to soup, roasted garlic lends a mellow sweetness, a warm note to add depth to the earthiness of potatoes. This soup is topped off with two wonderful things—a zesty arugula salad and addictive fried almonds that you will want to eat all day long.

1 garlic head
extra-virgin olive oil
6 cups (1.5 liters) vegetable stock
5 large potatoes
    (about 2¼ pounds/1 kg),
    peeled and diced
2 leeks, white parts only, thinly sliced
    and washed
2 handfuls of baby arugula leaves
handful of chopped chives
1½ ounces (40 g) Parmesan, shaved
juice of ½ lemon
sea salt and black pepper

FRIED ALMONDS

2 tablespoons sunflower oil (or other
    high-temperature oil)
⅓ cup (35 g) slivered or sliced almonds
1 garlic clove, very finely chopped
½ teaspoon smoked paprika
sea salt

Substitute

omit Parmesan for vegan

Preheat the oven to 375°F (190°C).

Take the whole head of garlic, slice off the very top—this will make it easier to get the roasted garlic flesh out—and place it in a small baking dish. Drizzle with olive oil and sprinkle with sea salt, then roast for 35–40 minutes, until the garlic flesh is soft and creamy. Allow to cool, then squeeze out the flesh from the skins. Set aside.

For the fried almonds, heat the sunflower oil in a small saucepan and add the almonds. Cook over a medium–low heat for 3–4 minutes, until golden. Take off the heat and immediately add the finely chopped garlic. Stir in the smoked paprika and add two good pinches of sea salt—you want it to be quite salty. Set aside.

Add the vegetable stock and potato to a large saucepan over medium heat and cook for 20–25 minutes, until the potato pieces are soft and ready to fall apart. Add the leek to the pan and cook for another 5–6 minutes, until softened. Add half the soup to a blender or food processor, along with the roasted garlic flesh, and purée. Return this pureed mixture to the pan with the remaining soup. Taste and season with sea salt and black pepper.

In a large bowl, combine the arugula with the chives, Parmesan, and a drizzle of olive oil. Season with sea salt and black pepper and add a squeeze of lemon juice. Toss to combine.

Ladle the soup into bowls and top each with a bundle of arugula salad and a generous scattering of fried almonds. Finish each soup with a turn of black pepper.

TIPS

This soup can be made ahead and stored in an airtight container in the fridge for up to 3 days. It can also be frozen for up to 3 months.

Make extra fried almonds and keep them in your pantry for snacking or topping salads and soups.

SPINACH AND ARTICHOKE CHOWDER
IN A BREAD BOWL

Serves 4

In the 1990s, eating out of a bread bowl was a big thing. As a university student, one of my signature dinner-party dishes was made by combining a packet of cream cheese with a few tablespoons of jarred corn relish and serving this in a bread bowl. Even though this dish eventually disappeared from my repertoire, it is still something I remember fondly. In America, it is nice to see that the bread bowl trend is alive and well. New England clam chowder is often served in a bread bowl—to the delight of my kids. This veggie chowder is a riff on spinach and artichoke dip, a pervasive bar snack in America.

6 medium round (6-inch/15 cm)
   bread rolls
extra-virgin olive oil
1 pound (450 g) cooked artichoke
   hearts (about 2 drained cans),
   roughly chopped
3 garlic cloves, finely chopped
4 cups (1 liter) vegetable stock
1 cup (250 ml) cream or nut cream
   (see page 130 for a recipe)
5½ ounces (150 g) mascarpone
½ cup (50 g) grated Parmesan,
   plus extra to serve
9 ounces (250 g) spinach leaves,
   roughly chopped
tiny pinch of cayenne pepper (optional)
handful of flat-leaf parsley leaves,
   roughly chopped
sea salt and black pepper

SPICY PARMESAN BREAD
AND PINE NUTS
bread from the hollowed-out rolls
½ cup (75 g) pine nuts
¾ ounce (20 g) grated Parmesan
tiny pinch of cayenne pepper
extra-virgin olive oil
sea salt

Substitute

canned artichokes: fresh artichoke
hearts
fresh spinach leaves: frozen spinach

Preheat the oven to 350°F (180°C).

Prepare the bread bowls by cutting out a circular lid from the top of each roll, lifting it off and hollowing out the inside of the roll to leave a thick ½-inch (1.5 cm) wall.

For the spicy Parmesan bread and pine nuts, tear the bread from the hollowed-out rolls into chunks and combine it with the pine nuts, Parmesan, and cayenne in a large bowl. Drizzle over some olive oil and season with sea salt. Spread the bread and nuts out on a small baking sheet. Roast in the oven for 12–15 minutes, shaking the pan once or twice during this time, until everything is golden and the cheese is melted. Remove from the oven and set aside.

Heat a drizzle of oil in a Dutch oven or saucepan, add the artichoke hearts, and cook over a medium heat for 3 minutes, until starting to color. Add the garlic and cook for 1 minute. Pour in the vegetable stock and cream or nut cream, add the mascarpone and grated Parmesan, and stir well, seasoning with a big pinch of sea salt and black pepper. Bring to a gentle simmer and cook for about 15–20 minutes, uncovered, to allow the soup to thicken.

Stir the spinach into the soup—if you like it spicy, you can also add a little pinch of cayenne pepper. Increase the heat, bring to the boil, and cook for 2 minutes to wilt the spinach.

Ladle the soup into the bread bowls and scatter with the spicy Parmesan bread and pine nuts, parsley, and an extra sprinkle of grated Parmesan.

TIP
For a sweeter soup, try coconut or almond milk.

COCONUT SOUP WITH ASIAN GREENS AND RICE NOODLES

Serves 4 / gluten free / vegan

For me, coconut is such an indulgent flavor. It is so richly intense, eating it feels like a sinful experience. I transgress often with coconut—coconut lattes are a common misdemeanor, along with bountiful bowls of Thai curries. This soup is a nod to these luxurious curries, an opulent coconut soup, lavishly decked out with snow peas and baby bok choy, and made hearty with rice noodles. This is a warming, cozy bowl for times when you just want to spoil yourself (and your family!).

extra-virgin olive oil

1 shallot, finely diced

¾-inch (2 cm) piece of ginger, peeled and finely chopped

1 large garlic clove, finely chopped

3 tablespoons Thai green curry paste

3¼ cups (800 ml) coconut milk (about 2 cans)

5 cups (1.25 liters) vegetable stock

1 tablespoon brown sugar

1 kaffir lime leaf (optional)

4 ounces (120 g) thin rice noodles, soaked for 15 minutes in warm water

6 ounces (150 g) snow peas, trimmed and halved diagonally

7 ounces (200 g) baby bok choy, trimmed and halved diagonally

sea salt

big handful of cilantro leaves, to serve

red chile flakes, to serve (optional)

crispy fried onions (store-bought), to serve (optional)

1 lime, quartered, to serve

Substitute

green curry paste: red curry paste

rice noodles: rice vermicelli, mung bean vermicelli, ramen noodles, udon, soba

snow peas: sugar snap peas, green beans

baby bok choy: any Asian green, such as Chinese broccoli

Warm a Dutch oven or pot over a medium–low heat. Once hot, add a little olive oil, along with the shallot, ginger, and garlic, and season with a good pinch of sea salt. Cook for about 2–3 minutes, stirring often, until the aromatics are soft. Add the curry paste, coconut milk, stock, sugar, and kaffir lime leaf, if using, and stir until combined. Reduce the heat to a simmer and cook for another 5 minutes, until fragrant.

Drain the rice noodles and add them to the soup. Add a few big pinches of sea salt, taste, and adjust the seasoning until you have a well-balanced soup.

When you are just about ready to serve, add the snow peas and baby bok choy to the soup. Cook for just 30 seconds, then take the pan off the heat straight away.

Ladle the soup into serving bowls and top each with some cilantro leaves and a sprinkling of red chile flakes and crispy fried onions, if using. Serve with a wedge of lime.

TIP

If you want to make the soup beforehand, don't add the noodles and greens straight away. Once you have the soup base, store it in the fridge for up to 2 days. When you are ready to serve, reheat and add the noodles and greens then.

LETTUCE AND BROKEN RICE SOUP

Serves 4 / gluten free / vegan

In Chinese culture, where it symbolizes prosperity and wealth, lettuce is always eaten cooked. It is most often stir-fried or served under braised mushrooms or tofu. It is also a hugely versatile vegetable, an everyday leafy green that is transformed into a celebratory dish and served with scallops during Chinese New Year. Cooked lettuce is wildly sentimental for me and eating it takes me right back to my mum's table. This recipe is a homage to a dish my mum would often throw together at the dinner table. Most nights, after a long day of cooking, my mum wouldn't feel hungry. So instead of eating the delicious food she had cooked for her family, she would take a bowl of rice, add some greens (usually lettuce), and top this with a clear broth or just hot water. This would be her dinner. Inspired by my mum's ad-hoc tableside dishes, this clean brothy soup is bulked up by rice that is cooked until it starts to break. It's deliciously simple, but so comforting.

extra-virgin olive oil
2 carrots, diced
1 celery stalk, diced
1 small yellow onion, diced
1 garlic clove, finely chopped
1 large potato, peeled and roughly diced
3 thin slices of fresh ginger
pinch of sugar
8 cups (2 liters) vegetable stock
¾ cup (150 g) white rice
2 dried shiitake mushrooms (or other
   dried mushrooms, such as porcini)
1 head iceberg or romaine lettuce
   (about 9 ounces/250 g),
   roughly cut into thick strips,
   plus extra to serve
2 tablespoons sesame seeds
   (white, black, or both), toasted
sesame oil, to drizzle
sea salt and white pepper

In a Dutch oven or large saucepan over medium heat, add a drizzle of oil. When the oil is warm, add the carrot, celery, onion, and garlic, season with a pinch of sea salt and, cook for 5 minutes, until the veggies are beginning to soften. Add the potato, ginger, and sugar, and season with sea salt and white pepper. Cook, stirring, for another 5 minutes.

Increase the heat, add the stock, rice, and dried mushrooms, and bring to the boil. Reduce the heat to a low simmer and cook, uncovered, for 20–25 minutes, until the rice is very tender and starting to break apart. Add the lettuce, cover with a lid, and leave to wilt for 3–4 minutes. Once softened, remove from the heat and discard the mushrooms if you like—although I like to eat them! Season with sea salt and a pinch of white pepper.

Ladle into soup bowls and serve topped with extra shredded lettuce, sesame seeds, and a small drizzle of sesame oil.

TIP

If you have leftover cooked rice, use it for this soup. You can also use brown rice, but in both cases, you will need to adjust the cooking time. The soup is ready when the rice is broken.

CAULIFLOWER SOUP WITH SMOKY EGGPLANT AND POMEGRANATE

Serves 4 / gluten free / vegan

Many years ago, I created a salad of roasted cauliflower served with smoky baba ghanoush, topped with pomegranate seeds and pomegranate molasses (the recipe is in my first book, *Community*). To this day, that salad remains one of my all-time favorites, an absolute triumph of texture and flavor. This is the soupy incarnation of that salad—creamy cauliflower teamed with smoky eggplant, topped with a few pomegranate seeds and walnuts for good measure. Baba ghanoush is one of my favorite food hacks, adding creaminess to just about any soup.

extra-virgin olive oil
1 garlic clove, chopped
1 yellow onion, diced
2 teaspoons ground coriander
1 teaspoon ground cumin
1 cauliflower head
    (about 1¾ pounds/800 g),
    cut into florets
5 cups (1.25 liters) vegetable stock
handful of pomegranate seeds
½ cup (60 g) toasted walnuts,
    roughly chopped
handful of cilantro leaves (optional)
sea salt and black pepper

SMOKY BABA GHANOUSH

1 eggplant
3 tablespoons tahini
1 small garlic clove, very finely chopped
1 tablespoon extra-virgin olive oil
juice of ¼ lemon
sea salt and black pepper

To make the smoky baba ghanoush, char the eggplant on the open flames of a gas stovetop, on the grill, or under a very hot broiler. Turn the eggplant until the skin is charred all over and the flesh inside is soft—if the outside is charred before the flesh is completely soft, place the eggplant in a hot oven and roast for 5–10 minutes, until it is completely tender. Allow the eggplant to cool for 5 minutes. When cool enough to handle, carefully peel the charred skin off the eggplant and place the flesh in a small bowl. Add the tahini, garlic, and oil and stir with a fork to break up the eggplant slightly, keeping it chunky. Squeeze over the lemon juice and season with a big pinch of sea salt and black pepper.

Heat the oil in large pan. Once warm, add the garlic, onion, coriander, and cumin, and season with sea salt. Cook for 2–3 minutes on medium heat, until the onion is translucent. Add the cauliflower florets and stock. Increase the heat, bring to a gentle, rolling simmer, and cook for 15–20 minutes, uncovered, until the cauliflower is very tender. Use a hand-held blender—or transfer to a blender—and whiz the soup up until very smooth. Season with sea salt and black pepper.

To serve, ladle the soup into bowls and top each with a big spoonful of the smoky eggplant and a scattering of pomegranate seeds, walnuts, and cilantro leaves, if using.

TIP

If you are short on time, use good-quality, store-bought baba ghanoush.

BURNT HONEY CARROT AND TAHINI SOUP WITH PISTACHIO DUKKAH

Serves 4 / gluten free

Carrot's versatility is often underestimated. A favorite vegetable in my salad making, here I explore the possibilities of carrot in soup. The preparation of these carrots is similar to when I'm creating them for salad, charring them to add smokiness and then lacing them with honey to add sweetness and deeper flavor. Finish with tahini for earthiness and a generous scattering of dukkah for a crunchy texture.

extra-virgin olive oil
1 ½ pounds (700 g) carrots, peeled and cut in half lengthwise
2 thyme sprigs, leaves picked
1 teaspoon ground cumin
2 tablespoons honey, plus extra to serve
1 garlic clove, chopped
1 yellow onion, roughly diced
5 cups (1.25 liters) vegetable stock
2 tablespoons tahini, plus extra to serve
handful of flat-leaf parsley leaves
sea salt and black pepper

PISTACHIO DUKKAH

4 white peppercorns
2 tablespoons coriander seeds
2 tablespoons cumin seeds
½ cup (75 g) pistachio nuts, toasted
2 tablespoons white sesame seeds, toasted
1 tablespoon black sesame seeds
1 tablespoon nigella seeds
1 teaspoon sea salt

Substitute

carrot: sweet potato
honey: maple syrup for vegan

To make the pistachio dukkah, place a frying pan over a medium heat and toast the peppercorns, coriander, and cumin seeds for about 60 seconds, until fragrant and popping. Add to a mortar and pound with the pestle to a coarse powder, then add the pistachios and pound again until chunky. Stir in the sesame seeds, nigella seeds, and sea salt.

Place a large frying pan over a high heat and, once hot, add a drizzle of oil. Working in batches, place the carrots cut-side down in the pan in a single layer and cook for 3 minutes, until starting to caramelize. Season the carrots with sea salt, scatter over the thyme leaves and cumin, and leave them to cook, without turning, for another 1–2 minutes, until charred on the bottom. Toss and cook for about 4–5 minutes, until they are tender, charred, and sweet. Transfer to a plate and drizzle over the honey.

In a large pot or saucepan, heat another drizzle of oil and add the garlic and onion. Cook for 5 minutes, until the onion is translucent. Add two-thirds of the carrots along with the stock and cook for 7–8 minutes. Remove from the heat and use a hand-held blender or food processor to blitz the soup until smooth. Return the soup to the heat, add the tahini, and season with sea salt and black pepper.

To serve, ladle the soup into bowls, top with the reserved carrots, scatter with dukkah and parsley, and finish with a drizzle of tahini and honey.

PASTA NIGHT

PASTA IS SOLIDARITY.

A bowl of pasta brings harmony to our family table, where approval is clear in the hungry eyes and smacking lips. Pasta is a staple dish for many families, and with good reason—it's a dinner made from pantry ingredients, it's simple and quick and, let's be honest, it's downright delicious. Like the noodles of my youth, pasta is an egalitarian dish that pleases and comforts. On pasta night, venture beyond Napoletana and Bolognese sauce, and unearth the possibilities of unique plant-based sauces (such as miso brown butter, creamed corn, herbed tahini, and caramelized onion with cashew cream) that will reinvent pasta night around your table.

My recipes are "choose your own pasta" adventures—mix and match your favorite pasta shapes with each sauce; use gluten-free pasta if you prefer. Just remember to keep a little of the pasta cooking water, as this magical starchy liquid will transform your dish, helping the sauce to cling to the pasta.

TOMATO AND WALNUT PESTO

Serves 4

Pesto is the consummate pasta sauce. With an ideal "just thick enough" consistency that clings perfectly to pasta, it is endlessly adaptable—I tend to make pesto with whatever leaves, nuts, and seeds I have on hand. Apart from classic basil, I also love to use spinach, kale, arugula, carrot tops, parsley, and cilantro. This pesto is a little different, with a bold tomato base. Grill your tomatoes to bring out their sweetness and add smokiness, then whiz them up with walnuts and Parmesan for a creamy, tangy sauce.

Recommended pasta shape:
fusilli / linguine / spaghetti / bucatini / pappardelle

2¼ pounds (1 kg) cherry or small tomatoes, halved
extra-virgin olive oil
2 garlic cloves, roughly chopped
3 tablespoons chopped flat-leaf parsley leaves
zest and juice of ½ lemon
¼ teaspoon red chile flakes (optional)
½ cup (45 g) walnuts, toasted
½ cup (45 g) grated Parmesan, plus extra to serve
1 pound (450 g) pasta
handful of basil leaves
sea salt and black pepper

Substitute

walnuts: almonds, sunflower seeds, pumpkin seeds

Heat the oven broiler to high. Place the tomatoes on a large baking sheet and drizzle over some olive oil. Season with a big pinch of sea salt. Broil the tomatoes for 6–8 minutes, until they have blistered and released some liquid.

In a blender or food processor, whiz up the garlic, parsley, lemon zest, and red chile flakes, if using, to a fine paste. Add the walnuts and half of the tomatoes and, with the motor running, pour in ⅓ cup (80 ml) of olive oil in a steady stream. When combined, stir in the Parmesan and season with sea salt and a good turn of black pepper.

Bring a large pot of salted water to the boil and add the pasta, stirring. Cook according to the package instructions until al dente. Reserve ½ cup (125 ml) of the pasta cooking water and drain the pasta.

Place the pasta in a large bowl and add the pesto, along with a splash or two of the reserved pasta cooking water. Keep adding the cooking liquid in small amounts until the sauce coats the pasta effortlessly. Scatter over the remaining grilled tomatoes and the basil leaves.

To serve, top the bowls of pasta with a generous amount of Parmesan, a sprinkle of lemon juice, and a final drizzle of olive oil.

LEMON AND PARMESAN

Serves 4

This pasta sauce begins and ends with lemon. Achingly simple, there is no "sauce" per se. Instead there are lemons, both juice and zest, combined with olive oil and generous amounts of Parmesan, which intermingle seamlessly with each piece or strand of pasta. Traditionally, lemon is teamed with spaghetti—spaghetti al limone—but I also like it with short pasta, particularly farfalle. This is a perfect one-bowl pasta dish.

Recommended pasta shape:
strozzapreti / spaghetti / farfalle / tortellini

juice of 2 lemons, plus zest of
    1 (optional)
7 tablespoons–½ cup (100–125 ml)
    extra-virgin olive oil,
    plus extra to serve
1½ cups (150 g) grated Parmesan,
    plus extra to serve
1 pound (450 g) pasta
handful of chopped flat-leaf
    parsley leaves
sea salt and black pepper

In a large serving bowl, add the lemon juice and slowly whisk in the olive oil until emulsified. Stir in the Parmesan and a pinch of sea salt.

Bring a large pot of salted water to the boil and add the pasta, stirring. Cook according to the package instructions until al dente. Reserve ½ cup (125 ml) of the pasta cooking water and drain the pasta.

Add the hot pasta straight into the serving bowl and, using tongs, toss through to coat the pasta in the lemon oil. Add a few splashes of the pasta cooking water to loosen up the oil.

To serve, scatter over some lemon zest, if using, and parsley and season with sea salt and black pepper. Finish with more Parmesan and a final drizzle of olive oil.

GREEN OLIVE AND BREADCRUMBS

Serves 4

This pasta sauce is a family favorite. The flavors are big, bold, and brash—briny capers and green olives share the limelight with crunchy toasted breadcrumbs and a handful of happy herbs. I encourage you to make this dish as herbaceous as you wish. Go even earthier and add some dill, tarragon, or oregano. I like Japanese panko breadcrumbs for their shape and texture, but you could go more rustic and whiz up some stale bread.

Recommended pasta shape:
linguine / spaghetti / fettucine / tagliatelle

extra-virgin olive oil
¾ cup (45 g) panko breadcrumbs
zest and juice of ½ lemon
1 tablespoon capers, rinsed and
  finely chopped
1 garlic clove, finely chopped
3 tablespoons chopped flat-leaf
  parsley leaves
3 tablespoons chopped basil leaves
1⅓ cups (240 g) green olives, pitted and
  roughly chopped
1 pound (450 g) pasta
1 cup (100 g) grated Parmesan,
  plus extra to serve
sea salt and black pepper

Substitute

panko breadcrumbs: fresh breadcrumbs
from stale bread, regular breadcrumbs
green olives: black olives

In a large frying pan over a medium–low heat, add a good glug of olive oil along with the breadcrumbs. Stirring constantly, cook for about 3–4 minutes, until the crumbs are golden, then remove the breadcrumbs from the pan immediately, season with a good pinch of sea salt and black pepper, and toss with the lemon zest. Set aside.

In a small bowl, add the capers, garlic, parsley, basil, and olives. Stir in ½ cup (125 ml) of olive oil. Combine well and season with sea salt, if required, and lots of black pepper.

Bring a large pot of salted water to the boil and add the pasta, stirring. Cook according to the package instructions until al dente. Reserve ½ cup (125 ml) of the pasta cooking water and drain the pasta.

Place the frying pan back over a medium heat. Add the green olive sauce, the pasta, and a few splashes of the reserved pasta cooking water. Toss, adding more cooking water if required, until the sauce coats the pasta easily. Add the lemon juice, a little at a time, until you achieve your desired citrus level. Finally, add the Parmesan, season with sea salt and black pepper, and toss again to combine.

To serve, scatter with the breadcrumbs, some more Parmesan, and a final drizzle of olive oil.

HERBED TAHINI AND PEAS

Serves 4 / vegan

My love for tahini originates in an unlikely place—*yum cha* (dim sum). Tahini is "Asian sesame sauce" by another name, a condiment that is widely used in Chinese cooking. At yum cha, sesame sauce is drizzled over pan-fried rice cakes to dramatic and delicious effect. Powered by tahini, this is a show-stopping pasta dish, creamy and flavorful, that will soon be on high rotation around your dinner table.

Recommended pasta shape:
spaghetti / linguine / orecchiette / rigatoni

1 pound (450 g) pasta
5 ounces (150 g) sugar snap or
   snow peas, trimmed
5 ounces (150 g) peas (fresh or frozen)
handful of mint leaves
juice of ½ lemon
extra-virgin olive oil
sea salt and black pepper

HERBED TAHINI SAUCE

½ cup (135 g) tahini
juice of ½ lemon
1 garlic clove, very finely chopped
3 tablespoons chopped flat-leaf
   parsley leaves
3 tablespoons roughly chopped
   mint leaves
1 tablespoon extra-virgin olive oil
sea salt and black pepper

Substitute

mint and parsley: basil

Bring a large pot of salted water to the boil and add the pasta, stirring. Cook according to the package instructions until al dente, adding the sugar snaps or snow peas and the peas for the last 30 seconds and cooking until the veggies are crisp and bright green. Reserve ½ cup (125 ml) of the pasta cooking water, then drain the pasta and veggies.

For the herbed tahini sauce, add the tahini, lemon juice, garlic, parsley, mint, and ½ cup (125 ml) of water to a blender or small food processor. Blend until smooth and creamy. If the sauce is too thick, add more water to thin it down. Add the olive oil and stir to combine. Season well with sea salt and black pepper.

Add the herbed tahini to the pasta and veggies, along with a splash or two of the reserved pasta cooking water, and toss together to combine. Transfer to individual serving plates and season with sea salt and black pepper. Scatter over a few mint leaves, add a squeeze of lemon juice, and finish with a final drizzle of olive oil.

MISO BROWN BUTTER AND CRISPY SAGE

Serves 4

Miso and brown butter is an unlikely pairing, but the result is rather earth-shattering. The miso adds a deeper savory note to the earthy and nutty sage-laced brown butter, coming together in a truly magical pasta "sauce." The miso brown butter can also be used as a dressing for roasted vegetables or grain bowls.

Recommended pasta shape:
strozzapreti / farfalle / linguine / spaghetti

1 pound (450 g) pasta
extra-virgin olive oil
2 shallots, thinly sliced
7 tablespoons (100 g) salted butter
20 large sage leaves
2 tablespoons miso paste
½ cup (50 g) grated Parmesan,
    plus extra to serve
3 tablespoons chopped flat-leaf
    parsley leaves
juice of ½ lemon
sea salt and black pepper

Bring a large pot of salted water to the boil and add the pasta, stirring. Cook according to the package instructions until al dente. Reserve ½ cup (125 ml) of the pasta cooking water and drain the pasta.

In a large frying pan over a medium heat, add the olive oil and shallot. Cook for about 7–8 minutes, until softened and starting to turn golden. Remove from the pan and set aside.

In the same pan over a medium heat, melt the butter. Once the butter starts to foam, add the sage leaves, reduce the heat slightly, and cook for 2–3 minutes, until the butter is browned and the sage is crispy. Remove from the heat, then take the crispy sage out of the brown butter and set it aside.

Immediately whisk the miso paste into the browned butter, until the mixture is well combined. Add the pasta to the miso brown butter, along with a splash of the pasta cooking water, the shallot, Parmesan, and parsley. Squeeze over the lemon juice, season with sea salt and black pepper, and toss well. To serve, add a final drizzle of olive oil and scatter over the crispy sage and extra grated Parmesan.

CARAMELIZED ONION CASHEW CREAM

Serves 4 / vegan

In recent years, I have become less interested in dairy-based creams and much more enamored with ones made with nuts. Cream of cashew is my absolute favorite, and I use it to make vegan mayonnaise, Caesar dressing, and "nutshakes." The magic of cashew cream is in its silkiness and sweetness; it is so good, I often substitute it for regular cream simply because I prefer it, and I have found that my carnivorous friends agree. This velvety pasta sauce is made even more luxurious with the addition of sweet caramelized onions and earthy walnuts.

Recommended pasta shape:
fusilli / linguine / orecchiette / angel hair

extra-virgin olive oil
2 yellow onions, thinly sliced
1 garlic clove, finely chopped
1 pound (450 g) pasta
2 handfuls baby spinach leaves
1 cup (140 g) walnuts, toasted and
    roughly chopped
3 tablespoons chopped flat-leaf
    parsley leaves
sea salt and black pepper

CASHEW CREAM

1 cup (150 g) cashews, soaked in
    1 cup (250 ml) of boiling water for
    1–8 hours
¾ cup (185 ml) vegetable stock or water
1 small garlic clove, chopped
2 tablespoons extra-virgin olive oil
pinch of sea salt

For the cashew cream, drain the cashews and add them to a blender or small food processor, along with the vegetable stock, garlic, and olive oil. Blend on high until the mixture is very smooth and creamy (if it is too thick, add a few more splashes of water). Season well with sea salt.

Heat a big glug of olive oil in a large frying pan over a medium–high heat. When hot, add the onion and garlic, and season well with a pinch of sea salt and black pepper. Turn the heat down slightly and continue to cook for 15–20 minutes, adding more oil if it becomes dry, until the onions are caramelized and sweet. Remove from the heat and set aside.

Bring a large pot of salted water to the boil and add the pasta, stirring. Cook according to the package instructions until al dente. Reserve ½ cup (125 ml) of the pasta cooking water and drain the pasta.

Combine the pasta with the cashew cream, caramelized onions, spinach, and half the walnuts. Toss and add a splash or two of the reserved pasta cooking water to loosen up the cream. Season with sea salt and black pepper. Serve in individual bowls and top each with a scatter of the remaining walnuts, some parsley, and a final drizzle of olive oil.

TIP

This cashew cream is super quick to whip up if you have pre-soaked cashews. I recommend soaking them in the morning, so they are ready to blend at lunch or dinner-time. You can even soak them overnight (use cold water, not boiling).

CREAMY CORN AND CHIVES

Serves 4

Inspired by the creamed corn of my childhood, this sauce is just heavenly. Super sweet and lusciously creamy, this perfectly simple homemade creamed corn takes about 15 minutes to throw together, even less if you use frozen corn (which is totally fine, by the way!). Top with plenty of Parmesan and a squeeze of lemon for brightness. For vegans, you could omit the mascarpone or crème fraîche and the butter, and just add a chunk of tofu—to add bulk and creaminess—and a few extra glugs of olive oil.

Recommended pasta shape:
linguine / spaghetti / pappardelle

4 large corn cobs, husks removed
½ cup (110 g) mascarpone or
    crème fraîche
1 garlic clove, chopped
2 tablespoons chopped chives,
    plus extra to serve
1 pound (450 g) pasta
1 tablespoon salted butter
extra-virgin olive oil
juice of ½ lemon
sea salt and black pepper
grated Parmesan, to serve

Substitute

fresh corn: frozen corn
(3 cups/420 g of kernels)

mascarpone: tofu

butter: olive oil

Bring a large pot of salted water to the boil and add the corn cobs. Cook for 2–3 minutes, until just tender. Remove the cobs from the water and place in a colander to drain. Reserve this pot of water to cook the pasta.

When cool enough to handle, snap the corn cobs in half and, using a sharp knife, slice the kernels off the cobs.

Place three-quarters of the corn kernels in a blender or food processor—reserve the rest for serving. Add the mascarpone or crème fraîche and the garlic and pulse until the corn is a coarse purée. Stir in the chives and season with sea salt and black pepper.

Bring the reserved pot of water back to the boil. Add the pasta, stirring. Cook according to the package instructions until al dente. Reserve ½ cup (125 ml) of the pasta cooking water and drain the pasta.

Add the pasta back to the pot and place over a low heat. Add the butter and pour the creamed corn over the pasta, along with a few splashes of pasta cooking water to loosen up the sauce. Toss well and season well with sea salt and black pepper.

To serve, scatter with the remaining corn kernels and a few more chives. Finish with a drizzle of olive oil, a squeeze of lemon juice, and a scattering of grated Parmesan.

VODKA, BROCCOLI, AND PEAS

Serves 4

Vodka sauce, along with Caesar salad, spaghetti and meatballs, and chicken parmigiana, is a great Italian-American invention. Italian food occupies a significant place in the American food psyche and while many immigrant dishes may have gotten a little lost in translation along the way, the dishes that have manifested are undeniably delicious. Vodka sauce, traditionally served with penne pasta, is a rich and creamy sauce with a signature pinkish, salmon color. The purpose of the vodka is a contentious issue, but most seem to think it helps release the flavors in tomato. Others say it acts as an emulsifier to keep the acid and cream stable. Regardless, vodka sauce would simply not be the same without vodka. It adds a bright bite and balances out the sweetness of the creamy tomatoes. Vodka sauce is also delicious as a pizza topping.

Recommended pasta shape:
penne / linguine / spaghetti / ravioli

extra-virgin olive oil
1 large broccoli head
    (about 1 pound/450 g),
    cut into small florets
1 pound (450 g) pasta
1 cup (150 g) peas (frozen or fresh)
handful of basil leaves
sea salt and black pepper
grated Parmesan, to serve

VODKA SAUCE

2 tablespoons extra-virgin olive oil
1 yellow onion, finely diced
2 garlic cloves, very finely chopped
1 pound (450 g) tomatoes,
    roughly chopped
⅓ cup (80 ml) vodka
4 ounces (120 g) mascarpone
½ cup (50 g) grated Parmesan
handful of basil leaves, torn
sea salt

Substitute

fresh tomato: 2 cans of diced tomatoes
vodka: white wine

Heat a drizzle of olive oil in a large frying pan over a high heat and add the broccoli florets. Cook on each side for 2 minutes, until charred.

For the vodka sauce, heat a large pan over a medium heat. Add the oil and onion along with a big pinch of sea salt, and cook for 5–6 minutes, until the onion is softened and starting to caramelize. Add the garlic, tomato, and a pinch of salt and cook for 1 minute. Remove the pan from the heat and add the vodka, then return the pan to the heat and cook on medium for 10 minutes, stirring occasionally, to allow the alcohol to cook off. Add the mascarpone and Parmesan and stir. Remove from the heat and add the basil. At this point, the sauce is ready, though if you prefer a smooth sauce you can whiz it up in a food processor or with a hand-held blender.

Bring a large pot of salted water to the boil and add the pasta, stirring. Cook according to the package instructions until al dente. In the last 30 seconds of cooking, add the peas to blanch. Reserve ½ cup (125 ml) of the pasta cooking water and drain the pasta and peas.

Add the hot pasta and peas to the vodka sauce, along with a splash of cooking water, and toss until combined. To serve, season with sea salt and black pepper, scatter with basil leaves, and top with the charred broccoli and extra Parmesan.

TIP

For a smoky flavor, you could also grill the broccoli on the barbecue.

GREAT BAKES

BAKES ARE COMFORT.

Deep-dish bakes are emotional foods. Reminiscent of home, they are dishes that make us feel comfortable, warm, and nurtured. My ultimate comfort foods are those that bring happiness to the table—mac and cheese, savory puddings, and creamy gratins that remind me of celebratory gatherings, and baked veggies that are beaming with flavor and sentimentality. Eating comfort food fills us with a certain solace, helping us feel connected to a person or memory, triggering powerful emotions and memories. Serving a great bake is akin to giving your fellow diners a big hug.

COOKING FROM SCRATCH, WITH JULIA BUSUTTIL NISHIMURA

JULIA AT 15 MONTHS OLD, WITH HER SISTER SARAH, BROTHER PAUL,
AND HER "NUNNU" (GRANDFATHER) AND "NUNNA" (GRANDMOTHER).
ADELAIDE, AUSTRALIA, OCTOBER 1989.

(OPPOSITE) JULIA WITH HER HUSBAND NORI AND SON HARUKI,
AT HOME IN MELBOURNE, AUSTRALIA.

Julia Busuttil Nishimura's life is lived slowly and simply, without the hashtags or trendy terms. She lives and cooks with an honest intention, a restrained purpose, and with robust integrity.

In her work, in her food, and in her person, Julia exudes a quiet sophistication that is disarming. Perhaps we can trace her innate sense of calm to her Maltese upbringing, rich in humble food customs—she spent many weekends in the family kitchen, shelling and drying broad beans, cleaning rabbits, and making ricotta. These simple rituals tied her to Maltese culture, but were also born out of necessity—during those days, without a Maltese migrant community in Adelaide, Australia, where she grew up, buying certain foods from the supermarket wasn't an option, so Julia's family had to make a lot of food from scratch.

Cooking food from scratch is a ritual that has clearly stayed with Julia. In her book *Ostro*, Julia effortlessly takes the reader on a delicious journey of simple food that is comforting and generous in spirit, a gathering of culinary inspiration from not only her Maltese roots, but also her time spent in Italy and Japanese influences from her husband. She is a natural feeder—her food is lavish and celebratory without trying to be.

Julia's earliest memories of her family table are of the formal dining table, where her mother cooked and served opulent dinner-party meals.

"One of my favorite memories is waking up to the smell of onions cooking. My mum always made French onion soup for the entrée and it would perfume the whole house from early in the day. Roast pork would follow and the meal always ended with chocolate mousse. There would be classical music playing and there was always a big emphasis on table manners."

In comparison, everyday eating at home was less formal. Daily meals included classic Maltese dishes such as oven-baked rice (*ros il-forn*), oven-baked pasta (*imquarran il-forn*) and rabbit stew (*stuffat tal-fenek*).

Her dad cooked Maltese ravioli (*ravjul*). Her school lunches were equal parts delicious and unique.

"My mum would pack me super-delicious but really typical Maltese lunches. A sandwich called *ħobż biż-żejt* was my favorite. It translates as "bread with oil" and is made by layering things like tomato paste, olive oil, tuna, capers, olives, and raw onion. All my friends had vegemite sandwiches and potato chips. I desperately wanted theirs."

At its heart, Maltese food is comforting. As an adult, Julia finds solace and joy in her early years spent learning cultural food traditions. Her memories of making ricotta at a very early age, perhaps at just three or four years, have left a lasting impression.

"I can see the bright red bucket we used to collect the sea water. The plastic colanders sitting on the sink and the warm curds tumbling into them. Maltese people *need* ricotta.

"My ricotta pie (*torta ta l-irkotta*) is essentially a celebration of those beautiful, rich, milky curds. A very simple but generous ricotta pie. You can also add parsley, broad beans, or peas, but I like it uncomplicated, especially if you can source fresh, high-quality ricotta. The pastry should be buttery and flaky and can be made without too much effort at all."

Ricotta pie is the dish that represents Julia's childhood. It was always on the table at family gatherings, and was the dish that welcomed her to Malta during her first visit as a teenager.

"It must have been nearly midnight when my sister and I finally arrived at my family's house in Malta, after a rather long train and boat trip from Italy. My aunty, who I'd never met, had a still-warm ricotta pie waiting for us on the table. She knew we would be tired and hungry and it really felt like a homecoming of sorts. In our family, that's how we show our love, through food."

MALTESE RICOTTA PIE

Recipe by Julia Busuttil Nishimura

Serves 6

With so few ingredients, it is crucial to use good-quality, traditionally made ricotta—it will make or break this dish. Traditional ricotta is made with the whey left over from cheese production and can easily be found in Italian or Mediterranean grocers. It should be soft and creamy, but also firm enough to hold its own shape when inverted onto a plate—be sure to avoid the whipped varieties that come in tubs and are far too smooth. If you don't want to make your own pastry, a good-quality puff or shortcrust can be substituted.

PASTRY

2 cups (300 g) all-purpose flour, plus extra
     for dusting
pinch of sea salt
1 cup (2 sticks/230 g) plus 1 tablespoon
     (15 g) chilled unsalted butter, cut into
     cubes, plus extra for greasing
about ½ cup (125 ml) iced water
1 large egg yolk, for brushing

RICOTTA FILLING

1¾ pounds (800 g) ricotta
2 large eggs
1 ounce (30 g) Parmesan, finely grated
handful of flat-leaf parsley leaves,
     finely chopped
sea salt and black pepper

To make the pastry, tip the flour onto a clean work surface and sprinkle with the salt. Add the butter and toss through the flour. Using a metal pastry scraper or a knife, cut the butter into the flour until the mixture resembles coarse breadcrumbs. There should be larger pieces of butter too, so don't overwork it at this stage. Sprinkle with iced water, 1 tablespoon at a time, until the dough just comes together, using your hands or a pastry scraper to bring it all together to form the pastry. I find I usually need the whole amount of water, but just go by how the pastry feels—some flours need more or less water. It should still be a little shaggy, with visible pieces of butter, as this will give the pastry its buttery flakiness when cooking. Shape the pastry into a flattish rectangle, cover with plastic wrap, and refrigerate for at least 30 minutes.

Preheat the oven to 400°F (200°C) and lightly butter a 13 x 9 ½ x 1-inch (33 x 24 x 2.5 cm) baking dish. Set aside. Remove the pastry from the fridge and briefly allow to rest at room temperature while you mix the filling.

To make the ricotta filling, place the ricotta, eggs, Parmesan, and parsley in a large bowl and gently fold all of the ingredients together. Season with sea salt and black pepper. It is crucial that everything is treated with great care here—don't beat the mixture, it doesn't need to be at all smooth, just be sure to evenly combine everything. Set aside.

Divide the pastry dough in half and, on a work surface dusted with flour, roll each piece into a roughly 14 ½ x 11-inch (37 x 28 cm) rectangle. Gently fit the first piece into the prepared baking dish and prick the pastry ever so lightly with a fork. Top the pastry dough with the ricotta filling and spread it out evenly. Take the second piece of pastry and drape it over the filling to create a lid. Trim both pieces of pastry so there is around ¾ inch (2 cm) hanging over the tin. Press the pastry edges together and, using your hands, fold them in onto the pie in a crimping action to create a crust all the way around.

Whisk the egg yolk with 1 teaspoon of water and brush onto the pastry. Make a few small incisions in the middle of the pie to allow steam to escape and bake in the preheated oven for 25–30 minutes, until the pastry is golden and the filling just set. Allow to cool briefly before serving warm or at room temperature. This pie is best eaten the day it's been made with a crisp leafy salad.

147

ONE-PAN SWEET POTATO MAC AND CHEESE

Serves 4–6

My friend-slash-culinary-wizard Samantha Hillman really changed my life with her mac and cheese recipe. There's no cream, no milk, no bechamel, no fuss. Sam relies on the alchemy of starch and water to create magic, producing the creamiest yet lightest mac and cheese sauce I've ever tasted. Using a tasty vegetable stock as the pasta cooking water is genius idea number one; then, there is the ingenuity of introducing starchy stock to cheese, a happy pairing that morphs into a rich cheese sauce. This is now the one and only way I make mac and cheese. This is a simple recipe with big flavors—the sweet potato adds an indulgent sweetness—and, best of all, it can be made all in just one pot. Minimal ingredients and minimal washing up.

extra-virgin olive oil
9 ounces (250 g) sweet potato, peeled and cut into very small chunks
⅛ teaspoon freshly grated or ground nutmeg
2 tablespoons (30 g) butter
1 yellow onion, finely chopped
3 thyme sprigs, leaves picked
1 pound (450 g) elbow macaroni pasta
5 cups (1.25 liters) vegetable stock
2 cups (200 g) grated sharp cheddar
2 cups (200 g) grated aged Gouda or Parmesan
handful of finely chopped chives
sea salt and black pepper

Substitute

pasta: gluten-free pasta
sweet potato: Brussels sprouts

Place a Dutch oven over a medium heat. Once hot, add a drizzle of olive oil, along with the sweet potato, a pinch of sea salt, and a splash of water. Cover and cook for 5–6 minutes, until the sweet potato has softened. Take the dish off the heat, add the nutmeg, and stir with a wooden spoon to break up the sweet potato. Remove the sweet potato from the pot and set aside.

In the same pot, add a little more oil, the butter, onion, and thyme and cook, stirring, for 4–5 minutes, until the onions are soft and golden. Add the pasta and stock and stir to combine. Cover and bring to a simmer, then reduce the heat to medium and cook for 6–8 minutes, until the pasta is al dente and most of the stock has been absorbed—you want some starchy water left in the pan. Turn the heat down to low, add the sweet potato and cheese and stir to combine. The heat will melt the cheese. Taste and season with sea salt and lots of black pepper.

Spoon into serving bowls, scatter with chives, and eat while still hot.

POLENTA WITH BAKED TOMATO MUSHROOMS

Serves 4 / gluten free

I have been making variations of this dish for years. There are so many elements that make this dish the perfect midweek meal—it's (almost) made in one baking sheet and there's not much chopping or equipment involved. It is really a case of letting the vegetables and the oven do the work for you. The cherry tomatoes and mushrooms shrivel and turn into a rich, jammy sauce. I have served the tomatoes with polenta, but you could also team them with pasta, rice, couscous, or a grain. If you are not a mushroom fan, I've also made this dish with tofu or even vegetarian sausages (if you are in the mood for that!).

1 pound (450 g) cremini mushrooms
2¼ pounds (1 kg) cherry tomatoes
2 garlic cloves, finely chopped
1 tablespoon balsamic vinegar
2 rosemary sprigs, leaves picked
2 thyme sprigs, leaves picked
extra-virgin olive oil
sea salt and black pepper

POLENTA

6 cups (1.5 liters) vegetable stock
1 ⅔ cups (250 g) instant polenta
3 tablespoons butter
3 tablespoons grated Parmesan,
    plus extra to serve
sea salt

Substitute

butter: olive oil (for vegan)

Parmesan: nutritional yeast (for vegan)

Cremini mushrooms: button, shiitake, or any other small variety

Preheat the oven to 400°F (200°C).

Place the mushrooms, tomatoes, garlic, balsamic vinegar, rosemary and thyme on a baking sheet. Cover with a good glug of olive oil, add a splash of water, and season with sea salt and black pepper. Toss thoroughly to coat the mushrooms. Bake for 30 minutes, remove the sheet from the oven, and give it a shake, then put it back into the oven for another 5-10 minutes, depending on how golden and sticky you like your mushrooms.

Meanwhile, make the polenta by bringing the vegetable stock to the boil in a large saucepan. Add a pinch of salt. Stirring constantly, pour in the polenta and stir for 3–5 minutes, until the polenta thickens. Remove from the heat and add the butter and Parmesan. Cover and allow the butter to melt, then stir to combine.

To serve, while the polenta is still hot, ladle into serving bowls and top with the tomato and mushroom mixture, drizzling some of the pan juices around the polenta. Top with more Parmesan and season with a pinch of sea salt and a good turn of black pepper.

TIPS

Any tomato leftovers can be repurposed as a beautifully intense chunky pasta sauce the next day.

If you have leftover polenta, transfer it to a shallow bowl and allow to cool. When cool, it will gel together like a cake. Cut into fingers and pan-fry to make polenta chips.

BRUSSELS SPROUTS GRATIN

Serves 4, as a side

A gratin is such a comforting dish, perfect for both everyday dining and celebration feasting. While gratins are usually based on a thick cream or bechamel sauce, I have lightened things up with crème fraîche, adding richness with two cheeses. To add character, I've accented the crème fraîche with my favorite warming spices—cinnamon, nutmeg, and bay leaves. Brussels sprouts rise to the challenge of usurping potato as the ultimate gratin vegetable. Their slight bitterness lends an undeniable sophistication to this simple dish.

11 ounces (300 g) crème fraîche
3 tablespoons vegetable stock
2 bay leaves
2 garlic cloves, grated
1 cinnamon stick
pinch of nutmeg (freshly grated or ground)
zest of ½ lemon
1 pound (450 g) Brussels sprouts, trimmed and thinly sliced
3–4 thyme sprigs, leaves picked
1 cup (100 g) grated Parmesan
1 cup (100 g) grated Gruyère
sea salt and black pepper

CHEESY BREADCRUMB TOPPING

3 cups (240 g) coarse fresh breadcrumbs
3 tablespoons butter, melted
3 tablespoons grated Parmesan
zest of ½ lemon
handful of chopped flat-leaf parsley leaves
sea salt and black pepper

Preheat the oven to 375°F (190°C).

To make the breadcrumb topping, combine the breadcrumbs, melted butter, Parmesan, lemon zest, and parsley in a bowl. Season with sea salt and black pepper. Set aside.

In a heavy-bottomed pot, add the crème fraîche, stock, bay leaves, garlic, cinnamon stick, nutmeg, and lemon zest. Stir to combine and season well with salt and pepper. Add the Brussels sprouts to the crème fraîche mixture and bring to a gentle simmer. Cook for 4–5 minutes, until the sprouts are starting to soften. Add the thyme leaves, along with the Parmesan and Gruyère. Stir to melt the cheese.

Pour the sprouts into a gratin dish, removing the bay leaves and cinnamon stick. Sprinkle over the breadcrumb topping and place the dish in the hot oven for 20–25 minutes, until the mixture is golden and bubbling. Serve hot or at room temperature.

BAKED SWEET POTATOES WITH LENTILS
AND CHILE—CILANTRO SAUCE

Serves 4–6 / gluten free / vegan

Growing up, my mum often professed her love for sweet potato. She talked about sweet potatoes incessantly and about how healthful they are and she was right—they're full of vitamins C and A. My mum would wrap them in foil and leave them to roast gently in a moderate oven, and then eat them as a snack. I didn't possess the same love for sweet potato until I discovered how wonderful they are teamed with olives. Sweet potatoes and olives are one of life's great pairings—like tomato and basil, chocolate and orange, macaroni and cheese. The sweet and salty juxtaposition is addictive. Use as much chile as you can handle.

4–6 small sweet potatoes, scrubbed
extra-virgin olive oil
½ cup (100 g) black lentils, rinsed
½ cup (100 g) green olives, pitted,
　roughly chopped
handful of cilantro leaves
3 tablespoons pumpkin seeds, toasted
sea salt and black pepper

CHILE—CILANTRO SAUCE
½ habanero chile, seeded and
　roughly chopped
½ cup (125 ml) extra-virgin olive oil
1 bunch of cilantro
juice of ½ lemon, plus extra if needed
1 garlic clove
sea salt

Preheat the oven to 425°F (220°C).

Place the sweet potatoes on a baking sheet and drizzle with some olive oil. Season with sea salt and bake for 25–30 minutes, until the sweet potatoes are tender—test with a bamboo skewer or fork.

Meanwhile, place the lentils in a pot and cover with plenty of water. Bring to the boil and add two big pinches of salt, then reduce the heat to low and simmer for 15–20 minutes, until the lentils are just soft. Drain.

Place the lentils in a bowl and add the olives, a few cilantro leaves and a drizzle of olive oil. Stir to combine.

To make the chile–cilantro sauce, blend the chile, oil, cilantro, lemon, and garlic in a food processor or blender until very smooth. Season with sea salt and adjust the lemon according to your personal preference.

To serve, slice each sweet potato down the center to create an opening and push the flesh down with a fork to form a well. Fill with the black lentil and olive mixture. Drizzle over the chile–cilantro sauce and scatter over the pumpkin seeds and a few cilantro leaves.

TIPS

To save time, use canned lentils.

Sweet potatoes are incredibly forgiving to roast, so wrap them in foil and add them to the oven when you are cooking other things. You can roast them for a longer time on a lower temperature, or for a shorter time on higher temperatures. Keep roasted sweet potatoes in the fridge for up to a week, for snacks and quick dinners.

GREEN BEAN TAHINI CASSEROLE WITH LENTILS AND CRISPY TURMERIC SHALLOTS

Serves 3–4 as a main, or more as a side dish / gluten free / vegan

Since we have been in America, our family has really embraced Thanksgiving, hosting many friends around our small table. I have come to adore this holiday—it's such a cozy and relaxed time of year, when we can gather to cook and enjoy great food and friendships, without the gift-giving frenzy of Christmas. Best of all, Thanksgiving is ripe with food traditions, such as sweet potato with marshmallow topping, pumpkin pie, cranberry sauce, stuffing, and green bean casserole. Green bean casserole is always on our Thanksgiving table—it is traditionally made by combining a can of cream of mushroom soup with green beans, which is then baked and topped with fried onions. Here, I've lightened up this dish with shiitake mushrooms, tahini, and homemade crispy turmeric shallots.

½ cup (100 g) black lentils, rinsed
extra-virgin olive oil
2¼ pounds (1 kg) green beans, trimmed
 and halved
9 ounces (250 g) fresh shiitake
 mushrooms, coarsely chopped or
 sliced
2 thyme sprigs, leaves picked
⅓ cup (90 g) tahini
juice of ½ lemon
1 garlic clove, very finely chopped
handful of chopped chives
sea salt and black pepper

CRISPY TURMERIC SHALLOTS

2 shallots, thinly sliced into rounds
2 tablespoons rice flour
½ teaspoon ground turmeric
½ cup (125 ml) sunflower or other
 high-temperature oil, plus extra
 if needed
sea salt and black pepper

Substitute

shiitake mushrooms: button or
cremini mushrooms

shallots: small red onions

rice flour: all-purpose flour

Preheat the oven to 375°F (190°C). Oil a large baking or gratin dish.

Bring a pot of salted water to a boil. Add the lentils, cover, and simmer for 15–20 minutes, until the lentils are just tender. Drain.

Meanwhile, make the crispy turmeric shallots. Toss the shallot rounds together with the rice flour, turmeric, and a pinch of salt and pepper, using your hands to break up the rings so that they are evenly coated. Heat the oil in a small saucepan until very hot (test with a wooden chopstick or wooden spoon; if it sizzles, the oil is ready). Add the shallot rings to the oil, a handful at a time, and fry until golden brown. When ready, place them on a paper towel to absorb excess oil and immediately sprinkle with some sea salt. Repeat until all the shallot rings are cooked. Allow to cool.

Heat a splash of olive oil in a large frying pan and add the green beans. Season with sea salt and black pepper and cook for 5–7 minutes, until the beans are tender and turning golden. Remove from the pan and set aside. In the same pan, add another drizzle of oil, along with the mushrooms and thyme, and cook until the mushrooms have turned golden. Remove from the heat.

Place the tahini in a small bowl, add the lemon juice, garlic, and chives and slowly whisk in cold water, 1 tablespoon at a time, until the mixture is the consistency of thickened cream. Season with sea salt and lots of black pepper.

Combine the beans with the mushrooms, lentils, and tahini sauce. Transfer to the prepared baking dish and bake for 10–12 minutes. Take the dish out of the oven, top with the crispy turmeric shallots, and return to the oven for another 5 minutes. Serve immediately.

TIPS

The crispy turmeric shallots can be made up to a day ahead. If you are short on time, buy ready-made crispy fried onions from your Asian grocery store or supermarket.

The green bean casserole can be made the day ahead and topped and baked with the onions just before serving.

Other high-temperature oils include peanut or rice bran.

BAKED POTATO, THREE WAYS

Serves 4

Potatoes are a crowd-pleaser with good reason—they are a humble ingredient, inexpensive, accessible, and incredibly comforting. The potential of potatoes as a complete family meal is endless, but the challenge is moving away from stodgy and towards nourishing and light. Baked potato is a dish I ate often for lunch in London. It was commonly served simply, with butter and lots of salt, or filled with baked beans and sour cream. With my baked potatoes, I fill them with lots of veggies and intriguing flavors. Lighten it up with tomatoes and mozzarella, spice it up with kimchi and cheese or go Asian with edamame, ginger, and scallion. You want to cook the potatoes for a long time—about 1½–2 hours—to get the crispy skin and fluffy insides.

4–6 large starchy potatoes
   (such as russet)
extra-virgin olive oil
butter
sea salt and black pepper

Preheat the oven to 425°F (220°C).

Wash and dry the potatoes well. Place the potatoes on a baking sheet, prick their skins all over with a fork, and drizzle with some olive oil. Sprinkle over sea salt and massage it into the skin. Bake for 1½–2 hours, until the potatoes are completely soft inside—test with a bamboo skewer or fork—with a crispy skin.

When ready, slice each potato in half lengthwise, add a knob of butter, and season with sea salt and black pepper. Serve immediately, or top with one of the delicious fillings opposite.

BAKED POTATO FILLINGS

Kimchi and cheese

For 4 potatoes

about 1 heaped cup (220 g) vegan kimchi
1 cup (125 g) grated cheddar
1 tablespoon finely chopped chives
sea salt

Fill each hot potato with a large spoonful of kimchi and top with a handful of cheddar. Return the filled potatoes to the hot oven and bake for another 10 minutes, until the cheese has melted. Remove from the oven, season with sea salt, and scatter over the chives. Eat immediately.

Caprese and pesto

For 4 potatoes

½ cup (125 g) pesto (homemade or store-bought)
1 cup (150 g) cherry tomatoes, halved
7 ounces (200 g) fresh mozzarella, torn into small chunks
extra-virgin olive oil
handful of basil leaves, torn
sea salt and black pepper

Add a spoonful of pesto to each hot potato and top with a few cherry tomatoes and some mozzarella chunks. Season with sea salt and black pepper and drizzle over some olive oil. Return to the hot oven and bake for another 10 minutes, until the mozzarella has melted. Scatter with basil leaves and eat immediately.

Edamame, ginger, and scallion

For 4 potatoes / vegan

2-inch (5 cm) piece of ginger, peeled and finely chopped
4 scallions or green onions, finely sliced
1 teaspoon sea salt
2 teaspoons tamari
½ cup (125 ml) vegetable or other neutral oil
1 cup (150 g) frozen shelled edamame beans

Add the ginger to a small bowl with the scallion, salt, and tamari. Heat the oil over a medium heat until it just starts to bubble—this should take about 3–4 minutes. Take off the heat immediately and very slowly add the oil to the ginger and scallion mix, taking care not to burn yourself, as the oil will spit when it makes contact with the mixture. Allow to cool.

Bring a small pan of salted water to the boil and add the edamame beans. Cook for 3–4 minutes, until the edamame beans are tender. Drain and refresh under cold running water.

Fill each hot potato with a small handful of edamame beans and spoon over some of the ginger and scallion sauce. Serve immediately.

TIPS

I always have a jar of kimchi in my fridge for snacking and last-minute meal ideas. Add it to noodles or rice for an instant meal!

Any leftover pesto can be kept in an airtight container in the fridge for up to 2 weeks or frozen for up to 6 months.

Leftover ginger and scallion sauce can be stored in an airtight container in the fridge for 4 weeks.

TOMATO COBBLER WITH BUTTERMILK PARMESAN BISCUITS

Serves 4–6

America has introduced many new culinary joys to me, and one of my favorites is the humble cobbler. In the warmer months, there is nothing that signals summer more than peach, plum, or berry cobbler—an oozy fruit concoction, topped with a buttery, flaky biscuit dough (American biscuits are essentially the equivalent of an Australian/English scone). I've learned to make a few different variations of cobblers over these past few years, but this one, a savory deep-dish creation of ripe summer tomatoes topped with a stunning Parmesan drop-biscuit dough, has become my go-to main-meal cobbler.

4½ pounds (2 kg) tomatoes
(any variety)
extra-virgin olive oil
1 red onion, thinly sliced
2 garlic cloves, very finely chopped
2 thyme sprigs, leaves picked
2 tablespoons balsamic vinegar
3 tablespoons all-purpose flour
sea salt and black pepper

BUTTERMILK PARMESAN BISCUITS
1 cup (150 g) all-purpose flour
¾ cup (110 g) cornmeal
3 teaspoons baking powder
½ teaspoon baking soda
1 teaspoon sea salt
pinch of paprika
7 tablespoons (100 g) chilled butter,
roughly chopped into large chunks
1 cup (100 g) grated Parmesan,
plus ½ cup (50 g) extra for topping
3 tablespoons chopped chives
1 cup (250 ml) buttermilk, plus extra
for brushing

Substitute

Parmesan: Gruyère, pecorino, or other sharp, hard cheese

Use gluten-free flour for gluten free

Preheat the oven to 425°F (220°C). Depending on the variety and size of the tomatoes, cut larger ones in half and leave cherry tomatoes whole.

Heat some oil in a large frying pan over a medium heat, then add the onion, along with a pinch of sea salt. Reduce the heat to low and cook for 15–20 minutes, until the onion is well caramelized. Add the garlic, thyme, balsamic vinegar, and flour and cook for 60–90 seconds, until the flour is paste-like. Add the tomatoes, season with a good pinch of sea salt and black pepper, and stir to combine. Remove from the heat and set aside.

To make the biscuits, place the flour, cornmeal, baking powder, baking soda, salt, and paprika in a bowl and whisk together. Add the cold butter and, using your fingertips or a pastry cutter, rub the butter into the dry ingredients until it resembles coarse sand. Stir in the Parmesan and chives. Slowly pour the buttermilk into the flour mixture, mixing with a fork or spatula until no more dry flour remains. Set aside.

Generously grease a large ovenproof dish with olive oil and add the tomato mixture. Drop large spoonfuls of the dough over the tomatoes, making six to eight biscuits. Brush the biscuits with a little buttermilk. Place the dish on a baking sheet to catch drips and bake for 40–45 minutes, sprinkling the top with extra Parmesan 5 minutes before the end of cooking, until the tomatoes are bubbling and the biscuits are golden. Remove from the oven and allow to rest for 15–20 minutes. Serve while still warm.

TIPS

This cobbler is delicious eaten the next day, so it's the perfect dish to make in advance. Once cool, store in the fridge for up to 2 days. To serve, reheat in the oven until hot.

Add some porcini mushrooms to the tomatoes for extra "meatiness."

LEEK, SAGE, AND GRUYÈRE
BREAD AND BUTTER PUDDING

Serves 4–6

As a carnivorous kid, my favorite part of rotisserie chicken was actually the stuffing. I guess this was a good indication of my future dietary choices. This bread pudding is inspired by the flavors of American stuffing, with sweet leek, earthy sage, and nutty Gruyère creating a beautiful mélange. Butternut squash with mushrooms, and kale with currants and pine nuts, are two other brilliant ways to dress bread pudding. This is also a great way to use up leftover loaves of bread.

extra-virgin olive oil
18 ounces (500 g) stale sourdough or country loaf, sliced about ¾-inch (2 cm) thick
2 garlic cloves, halved
2 leeks, white and light green parts only, thinly sliced and washed
8–10 sage leaves, coarsely chopped
1 cup (100 g) grated Gruyère
5 large eggs
3 cups (750 ml) milk or cream
sea salt and black pepper

Preheat the oven to 350°F (180°C). Generously oil a large baking or gratin dish.

Rub each slice of bread with the cut side of the garlic halves, then cut the bread slices into 1-inch (2.5 cm) squares. Place the bread in the baking dish. Finely chop the garlic.

Place a large frying pan over a medium heat, add some olive oil, and toss in the leek, garlic, and a pinch of sea salt. Cook for 7–8 minutes, until the leek is softened and golden in color. Add the leek, sage, and cheese to the bread cubes in the baking dish and toss well. Season generously with sea salt and black pepper and drizzle with olive oil.

Beat together the eggs and milk or cream and season well with sea salt and black pepper. Pour this mixture over the bread and leave to sit for at least 15 minutes (or longer—see Tip) to allow the bread to absorb the eggy liquid. Place in the oven and bake for 40–45 minutes, until golden and firm to the touch. Serve immediately.

TIP

This is a great dish to be eaten at brunch. Prepare the night before and let it steep in the fridge overnight for even more pudding-like results. When ready to eat, take it out of the fridge and let it come back to room temperature before baking.

HALLOUMI, KALE, AND MINT GOZLEME

Serves 4

At Australian urban markets and street fairs, a familiar aroma often imbues the air—the scent of sizzling *gozleme*. Gozleme is a traditional Turkish street food—these addictive flatbreads are filled with cheese and spinach (or meat), sealed, and then cooked over a griddle. They are my market favorite. My gozleme recipe is made with an extremely simple yogurt dough, which can be used as a blank canvas for any number of fillings. Melty cheeses with a green leafy veg work very well, as do pan-fried mushrooms with a fresh soft cheese, such as ricotta or chèvre. If you're after a hearty dessert, fill gozleme with Nutella and banana, or sautéed apples with salted caramel. I like to cook gozleme on the barbecue, but I've also made them in a sandwich press, on a stove-top griddle, or just in a frying pan.

YOGURT DOUGH

11 ounces (300 g) Greek yogurt
big pinch of sea salt
3 cups (375 g) self-rising flour

FILLING

extra-virgin olive oil
1 bunch of kale, stems removed
1 garlic clove, finely chopped
9 ounces (250 g) Halloumi cheese, grated
2 scallions, finely chopped
handful of mint leaves, torn
sea salt and black pepper

melted butter or extra-virgin olive oil, for brushing
1 lemon, cut into 4 wedges

For the dough, place the yogurt in a large bowl and stir in the salt. When combined, gradually add the flour, a few tablespoons at a time, until you have a stiff dough. Bring everything together in the bowl before turning it out onto a floured work surface. Using your hands, knead the dough until it is soft and slightly tacky. Place the dough in a lightly floured bowl, cover with a clean tea towel, and allow to stand for at least 30 minutes.

To make the filling, warm a frying pan over a medium heat. Add a drizzle of olive oil, toss in the kale and garlic, and season with a pinch of sea salt and black pepper. Cook for 2–3 minutes, until the kale is wilted. Take the pan off the heat and allow to cool. Once cool enough to handle, chop the kale leaves roughly, then add them to the grated Halloumi, scallions, and mint. Season with sea salt and black pepper and mix well to combine.

Divide the dough into four equal balls. On a floured surface, roll each ball into a 8–10-inch (20–25 cm) circle. Place some filling on one side of the circle and fold the dough over. Seal the edges with a fork (or crimp, if you feel like it!). Repeat until you have used all the dough.

Place a large frying pan over a medium–low heat. Brush both sides of the gozleme with melted butter or olive oil and cook on both sides until golden.

To serve, cut each gozleme into three slices and finish with a good squeeze of lemon juice. (I love lots of lemon on my gozleme.)

TIP

You can easily make your own self-rising flour by combining 1 cup (150 g) of all-purpose flour with 1 ½ teaspoons of baking powder and ½ teaspoon of salt.

ZA'ATAR ZUCCHINI AND MASCARPONE SLAB GALETTE

Serves 4–6

Galettes are perfect for lazy pastry makers like me! These free-form pies are defined by their lopsided, haphazardly folded pastry—this all adds to their rusticity. This pastry dough is extremely flaky, and the addition of cornmeal adds a pleasant crunch. For this galette, the thinly sliced zucchini means you don't have to precook the filling—experiment with other razor-thin seasonal veggies like potatoes, eggplant, or mushrooms. You could also fill this with seasonal stone fruit or berries for a sweet treat.

1 cup (220 g) mascarpone
1 cup (125 g) grated cheddar
1 large egg yolk
1 teaspoon milk or cream
2 zucchini (about 14 ounces/400 g),
  sliced into thin rounds
1 tablespoon za'atar
½ cup (75 g) feta, crumbled
sea salt and black pepper
handful of flat-leaf parsley leaves,
  to serve (optional)

CORNMEAL PASTRY

2½ cups (375 g) all-purpose flour
⅔ cup (100 g) yellow cornmeal
2 teaspoons sugar
2 teaspoons sea salt
½ cup (1 stick) plus 3 tablespoons (170 g)
  chilled butter, cut into
  ½-inch (1 cm) pieces
7 tablespoons (100 ml)
  extra-virgin olive oil
⅓–⅔ cup (80–170 ml) ice-cold water

Substitute

Use gluten-free flour for gluten free

Preheat the oven to 375°F (190°C).

To make the cornmeal pastry, add the flour, cornmeal, sugar, and salt to the bowl of a stand mixer and mix on low speed using the paddle attachment until combined (you can also use a food processor or mix by hand). Add the chilled butter and mix on low speed until it is evenly distributed, but still in large, visible pieces. Add the olive oil and mix briefly. Add ⅓ cup (80 ml) of the ice-cold water and mix—the dough will start to form. Keep adding more water, 1 tablespoon at a time, until the dough comes together. Place the dough on a piece of plastic wrap. Roughly shape the dough into a rectangle, wrap in plastic, and refrigerate for at least 1 hour or overnight.

In a small bowl, combine the mascarpone and cheddar. In a separate bowl, prepare an egg wash by whisking together the egg yolk and milk or cream.

Place the cornmeal dough in the center of a large sheet of parchment paper and, using a cornmeal-dusted rolling pin, roll it out into a large rectangle about 12 x 16 inches (30 x 40 cm) in size (make sure that when the edges are folded over the filling, it will fit into the baking sheet you are using!). Once you are happy with the size and shape, transfer the parchment paper with the dough onto a large baking sheet. Spread a thin layer of mascarpone mix over the dough, then lay out the zucchini rounds on top, overlapping them to create a pretty pattern. Sprinkle the zucchini with the za'atar and season with sea salt and black pepper. Fold the edges of the dough inward over the filling, pinching together any tears in the dough. Brush the egg wash over the exposed crust and scatter the feta over the whole slab.

Bake for about 40–45 minutes, until the crust is evenly browned. Slide the galette onto a serving board and allow it to cool for about 10–15 minutes. Cut the galette into pieces and serve with a scatter of parsley, if you like.

TIPS

The galette dough can be frozen for up to 3 months. To use, allow the dough to thaw to room temperature before rolling.

The whole galette can be made ahead and stored in the fridge for up to 2 days. When ready to serve, reheat in the oven or eat at room temperature.

CARBS WITH A SIDE OF *SEINFELD*, WITH LISA MARIE CORSO

LISA MARIE, PUMPED TO BE WEARING HER MOLTO ITALIANO DANGLE EARRINGS
THAT ONLY CAME OUT ON SPECIAL OCCASIONS, CELEBRATING
HER FIFTH BIRTHDAY AT THE CORSO FAMILY HOME, SEPTEMBER, 1993.

(OPPOSITE) LISA MARIE, AT HOME WITH HER MUM LORETTA, DAD FRANK
AND SISTER JUSTINE, IN MELBOURNE, AUSTRALIA.

Lisa Marie Corso is funny. Like, really hilarious. She is a comedy television writer after all, so making people laugh is her profession. But what isn't funny is her serious love of food. She freely admits that her brain is automatically programmed to think about what her next meal will be, while she's still eating her current one.

Born and bred in Melbourne, Lisa Marie spent her childhood eating her way through her Italian heritage. As such, she claims that her genetic makeup is "carb" and declares that food was the "lifeline of the Corso/Russo family and I am convinced our pores excrete extra-virgin olive oil."

"My grandparents left the old country in the 1950s and made a home for themselves in Australia when you still had to buy extra-virgin olive oil from the pharmacy. I am so glad the times have changed and you can now bulk buy it from the supermarket, then regret doing so when you realize there's no room in your apartment for a four-liter can of olive oil."

A common thread running through migrant families is an overabundance of food. Grandmothers who cater for five, but cook for twenty, and childhood memories rooted in food and cooking. Lisa Marie says her appreciation of her Italian heritage is 99 percent food related. As a child, she grew up devouring her dad's meatballs and pasta and her mother's *cotoletta*, and her family staged healthy debates over her parents' slightly different methods of making chicken cacciatore.

All nightly meals were served up alongside two crucial side dishes: *Seinfeld* and salad.

"My favorite culinary mash-up is a simple basil and tomato salad, with some Elaine Benes dancing."

Through all the humor, Lisa Marie's story of food is one that is common amongst the children (or grandchildren) of immigrants. Food becomes a vital link to understanding one's cultural backstory and cooking allows immigrants to protect and perpetuate an ethnic legacy.

For Lisa Marie, her love of food came from her nonna. She spent every school holiday with her grandmother, helping her in the kitchen and enjoying traditional meals that her nonna used to eat on her farm in Calabria in the early 1940s. Her time with her grandmother also resulted in some unusual, much-loved snacks.

"My favorite school holiday snack at my nonna's was crusty Vienna bread with her homemade pickled eggplant, which, let's be real, is a pretty weird snack for an eight-year-old to froth over."

For Lisa Marie, her nonna's eggplant parmigiana is the most primal kind of comfort food. Her recipe is a tour de force in cooking—it takes a while to put together, but the fruits of this dish are in the smashing flavors, and a feeling of nourishment that goes way beyond the plate.

"I really can't think of any other dish that makes me feel more content about life—individually crumbed and fried eggplant slices layered amongst a slow-cooked sauce and Parmigiano-Reggiano. Heaven is not a lifetime away, it's just a short two-hour trip in your kitchen."

EGGPLANT PARMIGIANA

Serves 6

Recipe by Lisa Marie Corso

SAUCE

extra-virgin olive oil

2 yellow onions, diced

2 garlic cloves, crushed

a sprinkle of dried chile flakes

a splash of red wine

6 cups (1.4 kg) tomato passata or purée (about 2 bottles)

1 bunch of basil, leaves picked and roughly torn (or you can use parsley if you prefer)

pinch of sugar

sea salt and black pepper

MELANZANE

3 large eggplants

4 large eggs

2 cups (140 g) good-quality fresh or dried breadcrumbs, plus extra if needed

2 cups (200 g) grated Parmesan, plus extra to flavor the breadcrumbs (optional)

pinch of dried oregano (optional)

olive oil

sea salt and black pepper

To prepare the sauce, pour a generous amount of olive oil into a pot over a low heat. Fry the onion, garlic, and chile together with a pinch of sea salt and black pepper until the onion is translucent. Add a splash of red wine to the onion and cook it off. Add the passata, then fill one of the empty bottles with water and add to the sauce (you may need a bit more depending on how thick the sauce is). Add the basil and sugar and bring the sauce to the boil. Simmer on low heat for 1½–2 hours. Be sure to check the sauce as you go—you don't want it to be super thick, as it needs to be runny enough to drench the parmigiana. Once ready, taste and season to your liking with salt and pepper.

Prepare the melanzane by slicing the eggplants into ½-inch (1 cm) rounds. Whisk the eggs together in a bowl and add salt and pepper. Place the breadcrumbs in a separate shallow bowl—you can leave them plain or add some grated Parmesan and dried oregano to flavor them. Coat each eggplant slice with the egg mixture and then the breadcrumbs, and set aside on a clean plate.

Once all the eggplant has been breaded, add a generous amount of oil to a frying pan set over a medium–high heat and allow the oil to get hot. Drop a test eggplant slice in—if it doesn't immediately sizzle when it hits the pan, it's not hot enough. Once the oil is hot, start frying the eggplant in batches for 2 minutes or so on each side, until cooked. Rest the cooked eggplant slices on some paper towel. (I like to clean the frying pan in between batches with a paper towel, so you don't accidentally cook burnt breadcrumbs.)

Preheat the oven to 350°F (180°C).

To assemble the parmigiana, take a medium-sized ovenproof dish and ladle in a scoop of the sauce to coat the bottom. Cover the surface with your first layer of eggplant (you want the eggplant to be tightly packed). Add more sauce on top of the eggplant so it's all covered and sprinkle over a generous handful of Parmesan. Repeat this method until you have reached the top of your dish—I like to save my "best looking" eggplant circles for the top layer. Finish with a generous amount of sauce and cheese and a sprinkle of breadcrumbs for a little crunch.

Cover with foil and bake in the oven for 1 hour, then remove the foil and bake for another 30 minutes so the top goes golden. Allow the parmigiana to rest for 5 minutes before serving, so it's easy to plate up. Serve with crunchy bread to mop your plate clean.

TIPS

This is an excellent base sauce to eat with pasta. Freeze any leftovers to make for an easy after-work dinner.

Demi, Dudley,
Juliet, Mandy,
Mary Tyler, Melba,
Michael, Richard,
Roger, Rudy Ray
& Thurston

FAMILY

ASIAN ROOTS

ASIAN FOOD IS MY HEART.

Eating it is intensely nostalgic, every bite is sentimental. My childhood was one ruled by food; one meal bled into the next. My mum is a rabid feeder. Her days were punctuated by food-related tasks—shopping for food, cooking, then planning for the next day's meals. She was relentless. The sheer gravity of food, the importance of each meal and the absolute sanctity of spending meal times together at the table are sentiments that have strongly shaped my approach to food. Asian food is generous and inclusive, made for sharing. From staple rice dishes to lucky noodles (symbolizing "long life" in Chinese culture), the intoxicating punch of ginger, the unusual preparation of vegetables (like cooked lettuce), and uplifting stews, Asian food never fails to boost my spirits and warm my heart.

FOOD OF LOVE,
WITH ERIN JANG

ERIN, BETWEEN 18 MONTHS AND TWO YEARS OLD,
WITH HER MOM AND OLDER SISTER, WON, SEATTLE, WASHINGTON.

(OPPOSITE) ERIN, AT HOME IN MANHATTAN, NEW YORK WITH HER
HUSBAND ABE AND HER SONS MILES AND NOAH.

Erin Jang has seen, first hand, the power of food as an expression of love. The child of immigrants from South Korea, Erin watched as her hard-working parents juggled several jobs alongside the demands of cooking hearty and delicious nightly meals. While Erin describes her homemade Korean meals as simple, it is awe-inspiring to understand how some cultures interpret simplicity in food—by today's standards, Erin's daily multi-layered fare would be deemed a feast.

"Growing up, my parents worked really hard to support our family. My mother held the night shift at the postal office when I was little, then in my high school years, my father had to work long hours. But my mother always made sure to have a simple homemade Korean meal for us. We'd have bowls of steaming rice, some sort of soup or stew, *banchan*, (several small dishes of marinated vegetables), and, always, kimchi."

Born in Chicago, Erin lived in New Jersey for a time, grew up in Seattle, and is now settled in New York with her own family. Food has played a strong role in connecting Erin to her Korean heritage. Erin has strong memories of the traditional Korean food she enjoyed growing up, seminal dishes prepared by her parents and grandparents.

"I cherished the rare times my father made a pan of kimchi fried rice. It would always be too spicy for me, but I loved how he let the bottom of the rice cook in the hot oil just a bit longer, to make it extra brown and crispy. We would just dig in with spoons and eat it piping hot out of the pan."

"And then there are memories of my grandmother coming to visit us in the summers and making wonderful meals. One extra special treat she would make was a sweet rice drink called *sikhye*. She knew it was my favorite, and she'd make a large batch, storing it in gallon-size glass jars in the refrigerator."

Erin, as with many children from immigrant families, grew up eating at abundant tables; tables where the food overflowed, barely leaving room for dinner bowls or cutlery. For migrant elders, particularly those with children or grandchildren growing up in

a culture different to their own, food is such a crucial form of expression, a way of showing your kids and grandkids how you feel about them.

"A memory I will always carry with me is a meal my grandmother made shortly before she died. I had just gotten married, and I wanted my grandmother to meet my husband; we flew to Chicago and made plans to visit her. She was frail and ill, but she surprised us by cooking a small feast. She had walked across the street to her plot in the community garden (she had such a green thumb—everything she touched flourished) and gathered vegetables and perilla leaves to make a special meal to welcome my husband. Her small table by the kitchen was covered with so many homemade dishes—humble, but delicious. Different kinds of kimchi, vegetable and tofu sides, beef she had marinated days before, the most flavorful stew—there was no room to even set down our chopsticks because she had prepared such an incredible spread. Even though my husband could not speak or understand Korean, he felt her love through her cooking, he felt the warmth and care as she nudged him to eat more. I understood in that moment how much love could be expressed through food prepared for others, how meaningful it can be to welcome someone to your table."

Now, as a mother to two young boys growing up in Manhattan, Erin keeps her Korean heritage alive by sharing recipes she learned from her mother with her family. *Pajeon*, Korean savory pancakes, is one such dish. Easy to make and endlessly adaptable, pajeon can be made with a plethora of fillings, from just scallions to seafood, kimchi, or any kind of vegetable. A simple dish that undoubtedly carries a lot of meaning.

"Most Korean families use *buchim garu*—a seasoned pancake mix you can buy at any Asian grocery store. But when I found myself wanting to make these for my own children, and didn't have time to trek out to an HMart in Koreatown, I started making my own batter from scratch. I like shredding up leftover vegetables we have in the fridge like carrots, zucchini, and red bell pepper, and sneaking them into the pancakes. The boys always gobble them up, especially when served with a dipping sauce."

VEGETABLE PAJEON (KOREAN SAVORY PANCAKES)

Recipe by Erin Jang

Makes 12 (2–3 inch/5–7.5 cm) pancakes

¾ cup (110 g) all-purpose flour
2 tablespoons rice flour
2 tablespoons cornstarch
½ teaspoon salt
1 large egg
¾ cup (185 ml) ice-cold water
1 small garlic clove, grated or
 very finely chopped
1 teaspoon doenjang (Korean fermented
 soybean paste) or miso (optional)
vegetable or canola oil

4 cups (800 g) finely sliced/chopped
 mixed vegetables (carrots, zucchini,
 red bell pepper)
1–2 scallions or green onions, thinly sliced
 lengthwise into 2-inch (5 cm) strips
finely chopped scallions, to serve

SOY DIPPING SAUCE (OPTIONAL)

2 tablespoons soy sauce
1 tablespoon rice wine vinegar
1 teaspoon sesame oil
pinch of sugar

If you are serving with the dipping sauce, combine all the ingredients in a small bowl and set aside.

Combine the flour, rice flour, cornstarch and salt in a bowl. In a separate bowl, whisk together the egg, ice-cold water, garlic, and *doenjang* or miso, if using, then add this to the dry mix. Mix until the batter is smooth.

Heat a few tablespoons of oil in a nonstick frying pan over a medium heat.

Now, there are a couple ways to cook the pajeon . . .

One way, which takes a little more effort, but looks really pretty (especially if you have an assortment of colorful vegetables), is to keep the vegetables and batter separate. Place a small handful of one kind of vegetable (for example, just the carrots) in the oiled pan, laying them down in a flat layer, about 2 inches (5 cm) wide. Then spoon some of the batter over the vegetables evenly, so there's just enough to cover them. Cook for a few minutes, until the bottom of the pancakes turn golden brown and crispy, then flip over. Add another spoonful of oil to the pan if necessary, to crisp the other side.

The other method, which is quick and easy, is to dump all the sliced and chopped vegetables and scallions into the batter, then fry spoonfuls of the veggie-filled batter in the oiled frying pan. Fry until both sides are golden brown.

Either way, I usually place a paper towel on a plate to soak up any extra oil on the finished pancakes, and then serve them immediately, scattered with scallions and sesame seeds and alongside the soy dipping sauce, if using.

TIPS

Doenjang is a Korean fermented soybean paste, similar to miso. It is optional, but it gives the batter a yummy umami flavor.

The dipping sauce is optional, as the doenjang, salt, and garlic give the pancakes enough flavor on their own.

I store leftover pancakes in a resealable bag in the fridge, and they can be crisped up again on both sides in a hot oiled pan right before eating.

You could use cooked leftover veg like roasted broccoli here; just nothing too watery.

STICKY RICE WITH HIJIKI, LEEK, AND CARROT

Serves 4 / gluten free (use tamari) / vegan

This dish is inspired by the flavors of *onigiri*, the triangular-shaped rice "balls" that are ubiquitous at convenience stores, mini marts, supermarkets and in school lunch boxes throughout Japan. I owe my onigiri infatuation to my friend Ebony Bizys (aka HelloSandwich.jp), an Aussie-born writer, photographer, and artist now living an extraordinary life in Tokyo. In this dish, I've paired a Japanese hijiki mix with sticky rice—otherwise known as glutinous, or sweet, rice. Growing up, my mother made sticky rice often. My favorite sticky rice dish (pre-vegetarian days) was served with diced potato, Chinese sausage (*lap cheong*), spicy dried shrimp (*har mai*), and shiitake mushrooms.

2 cups (400 g) glutinous (sweet) rice, rinsed and soaked in cold water for 2–24 hours

2 tablespoons sesame seeds (white, black, or both), toasted

handful of finely chopped scallions and cilantro leaves (optional)

sea salt

HIJIKI, LEEK, AND CARROT

⅓ ounce (10 g) dried hijiki seaweed, soaked for 30 minutes

extra-virgin olive oil

1 carrot, peeled and sliced into thin matchsticks

½ inch (1 cm) piece of ginger, sliced into thin matchsticks

4 fresh or dried shiitake mushrooms, thinly sliced

1 leek (white part only), thinly sliced and washed or 4 scallions, thinly sliced

3 tablespoons soy sauce or tamari

2 tablespoons mirin

2 tablespoons rice vinegar

1 teaspoon sugar, plus extra if needed

2 teaspoons sesame oil

sea salt (optional)

Substitute

sticky rice: white or brown rice

hijiki: wakame, arame

Drain the rice and place it in a steamer (see Tips). Sprinkle a big pinch of sea salt over the rice. Add water to a large pan to a depth of 2 inches (5 cm), cover, and bring to a rapid boil. Place the steamer over the boiling water—making sure the rice does not touch the water—cover and steam for 15 minutes. Remove the lid and use a wooden spoon to turn the rice around to promote even cooking. Check the water level—if it's low, add more water to the pan—then replace the lid and steam for another 10–15 minutes. Taste the rice to make sure it is cooked—if it is still hard, replace the lid and continue to steam for a few extra minutes, until all the rice is completely tender and translucent. Set aside to cool down.

While the rice is steaming, prepare the hijiki, leek, and carrot topping. Drain and rinse the hijiki seaweed twice under running water, then pat dry with a paper towel. Add a drizzle of olive oil to a frying pan set over a medium heat. When the oil is hot, add the carrot, hijiki, and ginger and stir-fry for about 3–4 minutes, until the carrot is half cooked. Throw the shiitake mushrooms and leek into the pan and toss everything together. Add the soy sauce or tamari, mirin, rice vinegar, and sugar, turn the heat down to low, and simmer for another 3–4 minutes, then add the sesame oil and mix well. Check for seasoning—you may need to add a little sea salt or a pinch more sugar. Remove from the heat.

To serve, spoon the sticky rice into a bowl and pat it down. Invert the rice bowl over a plate—so you are presented with a dome of rice—and spoon over some of the hijiki mixture. Sprinkle over the sesame seeds, scallions and cilantro leaves, if using. Serve immediately.

TIPS

The hijiki mixture can be made ahead and stored in the fridge for 3–4 days.

Sticky rice can be soaked overnight.

Sticky rice is best steamed using a stacking bamboo steamer, a fine mesh strainer fitted over your saucepan, or a stainless steel vegetable steamer (the kind that opens up), but you may also cook it in your rice cooker, as my mother does.

"SALT-OIL" RICE WITH COCONUT-STEWED SPINACH AND TOFU

Serves 4 / gluten free / vegan

Growing up, we ate rice every night. But it was never dull. The rice was the perfect counterbalance to my mother's big Cantonese flavors. Amongst the traditional Chinese banquet-style eating, there were several plain rice dishes that I always loved. I often craved her "salt-oil" rice—rice cooked in salted water and then laced with oil. She would often break an egg directly on top of the rice halfway through cooking, effortlessly creating a full meal. Sometimes she would serve "salt-oil" rice with garlicky *ong choy* (water spinach). I still adore this simple combo of rice with a sautéed green. This is my take on "rice with greens"—"salt-oil" rice with coconut stewed spinach and pan-fried tofu.

2 cups (400 g) jasmine or basmati rice
extra-virgin olive oil
12½ ounces (350 g) extra-firm tofu, cut into ¾-inch (2 cm) cubes
½ cup (65 g) toasted peanuts, roughly chopped
handful of chopped scallions or cilantro leaves
sea salt and black pepper

COCONUT-STEWED SPINACH
extra-virgin olive oil
1 yellow onion, finely diced
1 garlic clove, finely chopped
1 teaspoon ground cumin
2 teaspoons ground coriander
1 teaspoon smoked paprika
½ teaspoon ground turmeric
1 large tomato, roughly chopped
1⅔ cups (400 ml) coconut cream (1 can)
2 bunches of spinach (about 14 ounces/400 g), stems removed
pinch of sugar
sea salt and black pepper

Substitute

spinach: kale, chard, frozen spinach, watercress, ong choy (water spinach)

Place the rice in the bowl of a rice cooker or saucepan. Rinse the rice several times until the water runs clear. Cover with about 3 cups (750 ml) of water and add two or three big pinches of sea salt and a little olive oil to the water. If cooking in a saucepan, cover and bring to a boil, then reduce the heat to medium–low and simmer for 15–20 minutes, until the rice is tender and almost cooked (if it becomes dry at any time, simply add some more water to the pan). Turn off the heat, drizzle with a good glug of oil, and cover with the lid again, allowing the rice to rest for a few minutes (this resting period allows the rice to fluff up).

Heat a drizzle of olive oil in a large frying pan over a medium heat and add the tofu cubes. Season generously with sea salt and black pepper. Fry for 2–3 minutes, carefully turning the tofu often, until it is golden all over. Transfer the tofu to a plate and set aside.

For the coconut-stewed spinach, place the same large frying pan over a medium heat, add some oil, then toss in the onion and garlic. Cook for 1–2 minutes, until slightly softened. Add the cumin, coriander, paprika, and turmeric to the pan and cook for another 1–2 minutes, until the onion is fragrant and soft. Add the tomato to the pan and cook for 1–2 minutes, until it starts to break down, then stir in the coconut cream, fold in the spinach, and cook for around 7–8 minutes, until the greens are completely wilted. Add the tofu cubes and cook for another 2–3 minutes, until the tofu is heated through. Season with a little sugar and a big pinch of sea salt and black pepper.

To serve, dish up a bowl of salt-oil rice alongside the stewed spinach and tofu. Top with peanuts and your choice of scallions or cilantro leaves.

JAPCHAE WITH BRAISED EGGS

Serves 4 / gluten free (use tamari)

Japchae are sweet-and-savory noodles from Korea, a simple and traditional dish often served over a bed of rice to create a more substantial main meal. The texture of these noodles made from sweet potato starch is elastic, bouncy, and surprisingly light. My japchae noodles are given heartiness with braised eggs, which are also slightly sweet and intensely satisfying. We ate a lot of braised eggs as kids. My mum's vinegar-braised eggs—a traditional dish with pig's trotters, often served to new mothers—and soy sauce eggs were prized snacks.

11 ounces (300 g) sweet potato
   cellophane noodles
sunflower or vegetable oil
1 small yellow onion, thinly sliced
2 garlic cloves, very finely chopped
1 carrot, peeled and cut into thin
   matchsticks
4 fresh or dried shiitake mushrooms,
   thinly sliced
5½ ounces (150 g) spinach, stems
   removed and leaves roughly chopped
1 tablespoon sesame oil
2 scallions, finely sliced
1 tablespoon sesame seeds
   (white, black, or both), toasted
sea salt and white pepper

BRAISED EGGS

7 tablespoons (100 ml) tamari or
   soy sauce
2 tablespoons brown sugar
2 tablespoons mirin
1 scallion
4–6 hard-boiled large eggs, peeled

Substitute

sweet potato noodles: rice noodles,
mung bean vermicelli

shiitake mushrooms: cremini or
button mushrooms

omit eggs for vegan

To make the braised eggs, in a small pan that will snugly fit your eggs, add the tamari or soy sauce, sugar, mirin, and scallion or green onion with ½ cup (125 ml) of water. Bring to the boil, then reduce the heat to medium, add the hard-boiled eggs, and simmer for 15 minutes, giving the pan a gentle roll around every few minutes to coat the eggs. Remove from the heat and remove the eggs, reserving the braising sauce for the noodles. Allow the eggs to cool.

Bring a large pot of salted water to the boil and add the sweet potato noodles. Cook according to the package instructions for 2–3 minutes, until the noodles are just cooked. Drain and refresh under cold running water, then, using kitchen scissors, cut the noodles so the strands are shorter and easier to eat. Set aside.

Place a wok or large frying pan over a high heat and add a big drizzle of oil. Add the onion, garlic, and carrot to the wok, season with a pinch of sea salt, and toss for 2 minutes. Add the mushrooms and cook for another 60 seconds. Next, toss in the noodles, spinach, sesame oil, and about ½ cup (125 ml) of the reserved egg-braising sauce and cook for 1–2 minutes, until the spinach is just wilted and everything is well coated in the sauce. Remove from the heat and add the sliced scallion. Season with sea salt and white pepper.

To serve, divide the japchae among plates and add the braised eggs on the side, either halved or sliced up. Scatter over the sesame seeds.

TIPS

If using dried shiitake mushrooms, rehydrate them first by soaking them in hot water for 30 minutes.

The braised eggs can be eaten at room temperature or cold. Make ahead and store in the fridge for 3–4 days.

A LIFE LESS ORDINARY, WITH SZEKI CHAN

SZEKI AT THREE YEARS OLD, WITH HER OLDER SISTERS CHARLOTTE (LEFT)
AND CHARMAINE (RIGHT), OUTSIDE PIANO SCHOOL, HONG KONG.

(OPPOSITE) SZEKI WITH HER HUSBAND RICHARD, HER FRIEND SHIRLEY,
AND HER DOG, KUNA SCOTT, AT HOME IN MANHATTAN, NEW YORK.

Szeki Chan lives a colorful life. This New York-based fashion designer tells stories that are so unlikely that they simply must be true. Before she was Szeki, her name was Jacqueline. Jackie, for short. But as the story goes, Jackie Chan found it hard to compete with her more famous namesake. Hence, Szeki Chan was born.

Born in Hong Kong, Szeki attended high school and college in the UK, where she studied design and technology. After college, she returned to Hong Kong to become a pop singer. In her own words, she "failed." Shortly after, Szeki moved to New York, where she worked as a web programmer and a part-time street vendor. She sold handmade jewelery and "experimental" pieces at her eponymous store "Szeki," which she opened in 2008 on Clinton Street, Lower East Side. A couple of years later, this store morphed into "7115 by Szeki," which is now an iconic store on Rivington Street.

Szeki is an avid eater. Though she can sometimes go full days without food (she forgets to eat when she is busy!), she shows a childlike enthusiasm for food and cooking. Growing up in Western-influenced Hong Kong, Szeki's home life was a perfect mix of traditional Chinese with a few Western touches.

"In our house, the TV was always on. My mum always aimed to serve dinner during our favorite TV shows. Our evening meals were the typical Chinese banquet, usually four dishes plus a soup, and lots of rice. My mum was great at serving up a balanced meal, so she would cook a veggie dish, a fish dish, a meat dish and "go-with-the-rice" dish. I loved the "go-with-the-rice" dish the most—I had so many favorites: beef with cucumber, steamed eggplant with black beans, mango chicken cutlet, sautéed mushroom with tofu, eggs with tomato, and steamed egg custard."

At home, Szeki's parents loved to talk about food. Szeki was often their little helper in the kitchen, assisting in the making of her favorite dish, pig lung soup.

"It's a delicacy. This soup is, hands down, one of my favorite things to eat in the whole world. For years, I have been trying to get my husband and my friends on board with these lungs . . . so far, no luck!"

When Szeki talks about this unusual "lung soup," one comes to understand that her love for the soup goes beyond taste. For her, the preparation of the soup was a special time she spent with her mum in the kitchen.

"I remember helping Mum wash the pig lungs. It always made me feel so special to be able to help her with this task. First, we would stream water into the pig lungs and watch them inflate like a balloon. At a certain point, we would stop the water and then push the water back out of the lungs. We would repeat this up to 20 times, until the lungs looked completely white and clear. As a kid, it was the most magical thing to be a part of."

Today, Szeki's tastes have stretched beyond Chinese delicacies. When she was a teenager, she became enamored with steamed eggplant with black beans, a kind of "coming of age" dish.

"I didn't like this dish until I was a teenager, the taste is so earthy and it made me feel so "adult" to eat it. My mum and grandma both cooked this dish. It's just simple and delicious."

STEAMED EGGPLANT
WITH BLACK BEAN SAUCE

Recipe by Szeki Chan

Serves 2 with rice / vegan

4 Asian eggplants (or 2 regular ones)
1 heaped tablespoon Chinese preserved
   black bean sauce
2 garlic cloves, very finely chopped
3 tablespoons vegetable or olive oil

pinch of superfine sugar
2 scallions, finely sliced
sea salt
cooked white rice, to serve

Bring 2–3 cups (500–750 ml) of water to a boil in a wok or a large, deep pot.

Peel strips of skin from the eggplants, from top to bottom, so it leaves a stripy pattern.
Cut the eggplants in half crosswise and then cut each half lengthwise into four to six long
pieces (you want long finger shapes).

In a bowl, combine the black bean sauce, garlic, vegetable oil, and sugar. Spread the sauce
over the bottom of a heatproof plate—one that fits into a steam basket for steaming—and
layer the eggplant pieces on top.

Set the plate of eggplant into your steam basket and place over the boiling water.
Cover and steam for 15–20 minutes, until the eggplant is tender. Season with sea salt
and mix well to coat the eggplant in the sauce. Sprinkle with the sliced scallions and serve
with white rice.

SPINACH AND TOFU WONTONS WITH GINGER–PONZU BROTH

Serves 4-6

As a kid, I loved wontons. At *yum cha*, (dim sum) I would devour them deep-fried, smothered in a viscous sweet tomato sauce. At home, our wonton offerings were more traditional. My mum made them the signature Cantonese way, filled with shrimp and minced pork. She would make them in bulk and freeze them, making this a meal we could enjoy quickly, whenever the craving hit. This is my favorite veggie wonton—spinach and tofu. It is such an easy combination, with minimal preparation, yet is still packed with flavor. When picking your wonton wrappers, go for the square yellow egg variety (the round ones are for pot-sticker dumplings) as they are softer and hold up better to boiling. For the noodles, there is a variety called "wonton noodles" available from Asian supermarkets—they are chewier and more elastic than regular wheat noodles, but honestly, use any noodle you have on hand.

extra-virgin olive oil
1 garlic clove, finely chopped
7 ounces (200 g) spinach,
    stems removed
5 ounces (150 g) firm tofu, crumbled
2 scallions, finely chopped, plus extra
    to serve
1 teaspoon sesame oil, plus extra
    to serve
1 teaspoon soy sauce or tamari
2 teaspoons white sesame seeds,
    plus extra to serve
1 teaspoon potato starch or cornstarch
40–45 square wonton wrappers
8 ounces (240 g) wonton or dried egg
    noodles
handful of chopped scallions and
    cilantro leaves
sea salt and white pepper

GINGER–PONZU BROTH

¾-inch (2 cm) piece of ginger,
    peeled and finely grated
½ cup (125 ml) ponzu sauce
4 cups (1 liter) vegetable stock
3 dried shiitake mushrooms
sea salt

Substitute

wonton noodles: rice noodles, ramen
noodles, vermicelli

ponzu: soy sauce or tamari

TIP

Remember, always cover both unused
wrappers and completed wontons under
damp tea towels during the wrapping
process. If they dry out, the wrappers
will split.

For the ginger–ponzu broth, combine the ginger, ponzu, and stock in a saucepan and bring to the boil over a medium–high heat. Season with a pinch of sea salt. Reduce the heat to medium–low, add the mushrooms, and leave to simmer gently while you prepare the rest of the dish.

In a large frying pan over a medium heat, drizzle some oil and add the garlic. Sizzle for about 30 seconds, then add the spinach and cook for about 2 minutes, until wilted. Drain and, when cool enough to handle, squeeze out any liquid. Roughly chop the spinach and add it to a large bowl, along with the tofu, scallions, sesame oil, soy sauce or tamari, and sesame seeds. Season well with sea salt and white pepper. Using your hands, squeeze and knead everything together to form a coarse mixture. If the mixture is too wet, place it in a sieve and squeeze out the moisture with your hands. Add the potato or cornstarch and stir to combine (this will also help to absorb any excess moisture).

Set the wonton wrappers out on a work surface and cover with a damp towel—it's important to do this as they dry out quickly. Take one wonton wrapper and place a spoonful of the filling in the center—don't overfill; you only need a small amount. Moisten the edge of the wrapper with a dab of water and carefully fold one corner to the next to form a triangle, making sure you enclose the filling tightly to avoid any air pockets, which can make the wontons burst. Carefully pleat the two edges towards the center, to form a ball shape with a fishtail (a bit like a tadpole). Transfer to a baking sheet and cover with a damp towel to keep the dumpling from drying out. Repeat with the remaining wrappers. At this point, you can freeze the wontons, or just cook some of them and freeze the rest.

Bring a large pot of salted water to the boil, then reduce the heat to medium (you don't want the water to boil too rapidly as this might break up the wontons). Add the noodles and cook according to the package instructions until just tender. Place in a colander and refresh under cold running water. In the same pot, drop six to eight wontons into the water and boil until they float to the surface. Remove immediately from the water with a slotted spoon and set aside. Continue until all the wontons are cooked.

To serve, place the noodles in deep serving bowls, top with five to eight wontons, and add a small ladleful of the ponzu broth to just cover the wontons. Top each bowl with some chopped scallions, cilantro leaves, and a scattering of sesame seeds. Serve immediately.

FIVE-SPICE CAULIFLOWER STEAKS
WITH MUSHROOM "XO" SAUCE

Serves 4 / gluten free (use tamari) / vegan

Growing up, we ate chile with everything. My mum grew her own bird's eye chiles so the only heat gauge we knew was extra hot. Her homemade chile sauce was vibrantly red and acidic, replicating our favorite commercial brand, Koon Yick Chile Sauce, which is served at most Cantonese restaurants and at *yum cha*, or dim sum. We didn't eat XO sauce until we were much older. XO isn't really a chile sauce, but rather a spicy seafood sauce comprised of prized Chinese ingredients—scallops, dried fish, and shrimp—and subsequently cooked with chiles, onions, and garlic. For vegetarians, being without XO is not fun. However, this mushroom version, brimming with the umami goodness of shiitake mushrooms, satisfies all my XO cravings. It's intense and heady, and I want to eat it with everything.

2 cauliflower heads
  (about 3¾ pounds/1.6 kg)
extra-virgin olive oil
2 teaspoons five-spice powder
handful of cilantro leaves or
  chopped scallions
sea salt
cooked white rice, to serve

MUSHROOM "XO" SAUCE

2 teaspoons hijiki seaweed, soaked in
  hot water for 20 minutes
⅓ cup (80 ml) olive oil or sunflower oil
3 tablespoons tamari or soy sauce
2 garlic cloves, very finely chopped
1 scallion, very finely chopped
5 ounces (150 g) fresh or dried shiitake
  mushrooms, finely chopped
1–2 whole dried chiles (or 1 teaspoon
  red chile flakes), broken into
  small pieces
¾-inch (2 cm) piece of ginger,
  very finely chopped
1 cinnamon stick
1 star anise
black pepper

Substitute

cauliflower: eggplant, Brussels sprouts,
broccoli, green beans

shiitake mushrooms: cremini
mushrooms, dried and rehydrated
shiitake mushrooms

dried chiles: fresh chiles

Preheat the oven to 400°F (200°C).

Carefully slice the cauliflowers into ½-inch (1.25 cm) thick "steaks." Lay out the cauliflower steaks—including any florets that have dropped off—on two large baking sheets and drizzle them with olive oil. Scatter over some sea salt and the five-spice powder. Roast in the oven for 25–30 minutes, until the cauliflower steaks are golden on the outside and tender on the inside.

Meanwhile, for the mushroom "XO" sauce, drain the hijiki and dry with paper towels. In a large frying pan or wok, heat the oil and tamari or soy sauce over a medium–low heat. When warm but not boiling, add the garlic and scallion and cook for 2 minutes. Add the mushrooms, chile, ginger, hijiki, cinnamon, star anise, and a good turn of black pepper and leave to cook for 10 minutes on a very low heat, until the mushrooms have softened and the mixture has reduced and thickened. Take off the heat and remove the cinnamon stick and star anise.

To serve, place the cauliflower "steaks" on a serving platter, spoon over a generous amount of mushroom "XO" sauce, and scatter over the cilantro leaves or chopped scallions. Serve with white rice.

TIPS

If using dried shiitake mushrooms, rehydrate them first by soaking them in hot water for 30 minutes.

You can make the mushroom "XO" sauce ahead of time and store it in an airtight container in the fridge until needed (it will keep for up to 1 week).

The mushroom "XO" sauce is also an excellent topping for the sticky rice on page 195.

STIR-FRIED LETTUCE BOWL WITH GINGER FRIED RICE AND FRIED EGG

Serves 4

This bowl is a snapshot of how our family ate growing up. Pared back flavors of ginger, both dominant and delicate, permeating each simple dish in a bold yet subtle way. Ginger fried rice is my comfort food in every sense—my mum made this for me whenever I was feeling unwell; the dish is particularly good for settling a restless tummy and is also a proficient hangover cure. Ginger is a hugely nostalgic ingredient for me—it is the smell I associate most with my mother, a smell that was always present on her hardworking hands. It is a smell that brings me much comfort in the kitchen.

1 iceberg lettuce head
 (1 ¾ pound/750 g)
1 tablespoon tamari or soy sauce
2 teaspoons hoisin sauce
1 tablespoon sesame oil
¼ teaspoon sugar
extra-virgin olive oil or sunflower oil
¾-inch (2 cm) piece of ginger, peeled
 and finely chopped
1 garlic clove, finely chopped
4–6 large eggs
4 scallions, finely chopped
2 tablespoons sesame seeds
 (white, black, or both), toasted
sea salt and white pepper

GINGER FRIED RICE

extra-virgin olive oil or sunflower oil
2-inch (5 cm) piece of ginger, peeled and
 finely chopped
5 cups (925 g) cooked cold brown rice
sea salt and white pepper

Substitute

iceberg lettuce: romaine lettuce,
cabbage

hoisin sauce: vegetarian oyster sauce,
kecap manis, soy sauce

omit eggs for vegan

To remove the core of the lettuce, take a sharp paring knife, run it around the core, and then gently pull it out. Remove the outer layer of the lettuce and discard. Now tear the lettuce into large chunks. Wash the leaves and allow them to dry in a colander.

In a small bowl, whisk together the tamari or soy sauce, hoisin sauce, sesame oil, sugar, and a pinch of sea salt and white pepper. Set sauce aside.

Heat a large frying pan or wok over a medium–low heat, add a drizzle of oil, along with the ginger and garlic, and cook for 30 seconds. Increase the heat to medium, add the lettuce, and stir-fry for 1–2 minutes, until the lettuce is wilted. Pour the sauce over the lettuce and stir-fry for a further 60 seconds. Take care not to overcook, as you want the lettuce to retain some crunch. Remove from the pan and set aside. Once the pan is cool enough to handle, rinse it out and dry.

For the ginger fried rice, reheat the pan on high heat and add a good drizzle of oil. Toss in the ginger and cook for 30 seconds, then add the cold rice and stir-fry for 4–5 minutes, until the rice is heated through. Season with sea salt and a small pinch of white pepper, then remove from the pan and set aside.

Wipe the pan clean once again and place over a medium–high heat. Add another drizzle of oil and add 1 egg to the pan (cook 1 egg at a time). Season the egg with a touch of salt and immediately cover with a lid. Cook until the white is just set and the yolk is to your liking. Repeat with all the eggs.

To serve, scoop the ginger fried rice into individual serving bowls and top each with the stir-fried lettuce and a fried egg. Scatter with the scallions and sesame seeds and season with a little sea salt and white pepper.

KOREAN SILKEN TOFU STEW

Serves 4 / gluten free

I am a latecomer to Korean food. I never really experienced great Korean food until I moved to New York. I owe my Korean food epiphany to many local friends who opened my eyes to the world of intensely flavorful kimchi, *japchae*, kimchi pancakes, rice cakes, and *bibimbap*. My friend CC Malerba coaches me about the food she ate growing up; I am her diligent student. She introduced me to a tofu house called BCD Tofu in Koreatown, Manhattan. On our first visit, I noticed that the predominantly Korean crowd were all eating the same dish—a pot of tofu, with various toppings, and an egg, which they would break straight into the hot stew. Once I experienced this bowl of "*soon* tofu" (soft tofu) for myself, there was no turning back. This is the silkiest tofu I've ever eaten. My daughter declared it her "favorite dish ever." This is my vegetarian version.

1 tablespoon sesame oil
2 garlic cloves, finely chopped
½ yellow onion, thinly sliced
½ cup (120 g) vegan kimchi, roughly
    chopped, plus extra to serve
1–2 teaspoons gochujang (Korean
    fermented hot pepper paste)
4 fresh or dried shiitake mushrooms,
    thinly sliced
25 ounces (700 g) silken tofu
1¾ ounces (50 g) enoki mushrooms,
    trimmed
3 scallions, finely chopped
4 large eggs
white rice, to serve

UMAMI BROTH

1 large piece of dried kombu or
    wakame seaweed
    (about 8 x 4 inches/20 x 10 cm)
3 dried shiitake mushrooms
4 cups (1 liter) vegetable stock
½ yellow onion

Substitute

gochujang (Korean fermented hot
pepper paste): sriracha (see Tips)

omit eggs for vegan

For the umami broth, place all the ingredients in a large saucepan and bring to the boil. Turn the heat down to medium–low and simmer for 15–20 minutes. Strain the broth—you should be left with about 2 cups (500 ml) of broth.

Drizzle some sesame oil into a Dutch oven or heavy-bottomed pot— ideally one that can be brought to the table to serve—and sauté the garlic, onion, and kimchi over medium heat for about 1–2 minutes, until everything is well coated and starting to soften. Add the strained broth along with the gochujang and shiitake mushrooms, and increase the heat to bring it to a boil. Stir the tofu into the stew and, using a large metal spoon, carefully break it up into bite-sized pieces. Allow the stew to simmer on medium–high heat for 15–20 minutes, to allow the flavors to develop and the stew to thicken up.

Just before serving, increase the heat to high until the mixture starts to rapidly bubble. Top the stew with the enoki mushrooms and scallions and then crack the eggs, 1 at a time, straight into the stew.

Bring the pot to the table and enjoy family-style, with a side of white rice and extra kimchi (if you like).

TIPS

If using dried shiitake mushrooms, rehydrate them first by soaking them in hot water for 30 minutes.

Gochujang can be found at Asian grocers and in the Asian aisle of regular supermarkets. If you can't find it, add a dash of Sriracha mixed with soy sauce and a pinch of sugar instead.

Always adjust the level of heat according to your family's tastes. Kimchi is traditionally very spicy, so you might want to choose one that is mild.

Even though you may not think of kimchi as a food for younger palates, I have found many kids love its funky taste, so don't be afraid to try this with your family. You may be surprised. My friend CC Malerba tells me that, when she was a kid, her mum used to rinse kimchi in water just to remove the chile flakes before serving; reducing some of the spice, but retaining the "fermented" flavor. An excellent tip.

FROM BANGALORE TO BROOKLYN, WITH CHITRA AGRAWAL

FROM LEFT TO RIGHT: CHITRA'S BROTHER, VIKAS, HER DAD, VISHWANI,
CHITRA AND HER MOM, PRATHIMA, NEW JERSEY, CIRCA 1982.

(OPPOSITE) CHITRA AND HER HUSBAND BEN IN THEIR BROOKLYN HOME.

Chitra Agrawal calls herself an American Born Confused Desi, a term commonly used to describe a "desi" or South Asian born and brought up in the US. In Chitra's case, she is of Indian descent, born in New Jersey, raised in California, and now settled in Brooklyn, New York. While labels can be hard to shake, for Chitra, this cultural disparity was her fuel. In 2009, she started her inspiring blog, *The ABCDs of Cooking*, a journal of vegetarian recipes rooted in traditional Indian cooking and reflective of Indian diaspora. She also channels her heritage into Brooklyn Delhi, her line of premium achaars, an Indian pantry staple.

Chitra's food is what modern American cuisine should be—traditional with a nod to modernism, respectful of cultural customs and celebratory of time-honored rituals. Her first book, *Vibrant India*, is a beautiful, evocative ode to her mother and her hometown of Bangalore, an exploration of the spirited food traditions of South Indian cooking.

Growing up, Chitra savored the diverse cuisine of India.

"My mother is from South India so she makes more rice, lentils, fresh veg salads and dishes, flavored with black mustard seeds, curry leaves, yogurt, and coconut. My father is from North India and he would make the breads and curries, much of the food you find in the restaurants but not as heavy since he doesn't cook with ghee or cream. He also is the yogurt maker in the family nowadays. Our meals were always a mix of their cuisines. We may have a chitranna, lemon rice flavored with fried peanuts, coconut, and fried spices; refreshing yogurt raita; *saaru*, a spicy and sour tomato-and-lentil soup; chapatti, thin flatbread made from durum wheat; and chana masala, or chickpea curry. It's hard to pick my favorite dish growing up, as I loved the food both my parents made. I loved my father's palak paneer

and my mother's *majjige huli*, which is a coconut yogurt curry made with a watery vegetable like chayote squash and flavored with green chile peppers and coriander."

For this lifelong vegetarian, the markets of America and India provide beautiful produce for vegetable-packed dishes, along with a few special food memories with her family.

"My parents are meticulous about their vegetable and fruit shopping. I can remember shopping in both the US and in India with them as they would carefully pick out produce at the markets for the day's cooking. When they come to visit in Brooklyn, I most enjoy our daily visits to the grocer—each morning my father will expertly peel and cut fresh fruits like melon or papaya into perfect squares. In the summers growing up, he would cut mango for the family each evening after dinner. So delicious!"

While her parents have fostered a deep love of food, Chitra also learns a lot about cooking from her great aunt, whom she visits regularly in Delhi. Chitra's chana masala is inspired by a recipe from her great aunt. It's not your standard chickpea curry, but one that is flavored with tea, cinnamon, bay leaves, and cloves. It has sour notes from the addition of amchoor powder (dried mango powder).

Chitra and her great aunt's relationship is one of relishing nature and the simple rituals of home cooking.

"In the mornings, we go walking in Deer Park or the Rose Garden close by to her home. We walk very early so you can see the morning mist rising. The trees and greenery look just magical at that hour. On our way home, right outside of the park, we shop for vegetables for cooking that day. I look forward to this daily ritual when visiting India."

MY GREAT AUNT'S CHANA MASALA

Recipe by Chitra Agrawal

Serves 4 / vegan (use oil)

1¼ pounds (500 g) cooked chickpeas
    (about 2 drained cans)
1 black tea bag
1 cinnamon stick
1 bay leaf
2 cardamom pods
2 tablespoons ghee or oil
1 teaspoon cumin seeds
pinch of asafetida
1 red onion, diced
1 tablespoon grated ginger
1 garlic clove, very finely chopped
1 Indian green chile or serrano chile,
    very finely chopped

3 tablespoons tomato passata or purée
1 tablespoon ground coriander
½ teaspoon amchoor (dried mango powder)
½ teaspoon ground cumin
¼ teaspoon ground turmeric
¼ teaspoon garam masala, plus extra
    to serve
¼ teaspoon Indian chile powder
    or cayenne pepper (or to taste)
sea salt
handful of chopped cilantro, to serve
cooked rice or flatbread, to serve

Strain the chickpeas and rinse with water.

In a large pot, add the chickpeas, tea bag, cinnamon stick, bay leaf, cardamom pods, and 6 cups (1.5 liters) of water, bring to a boil, then reduce the heat and simmer for about 10–15 minutes. Remove from the heat and set aside. (This is usually done with dried chickpeas, but after trying it with canned chickpeas, I liked how soft they got and how the liquid gently flavored the chickpeas). I like to keep the cooking water so I can add some to the curry for more flavor.

In a large frying pan, heat the ghee or oil over a medium–high heat. Once hot, add the cumin seeds and asafetida and give the pan a shake so they mingle. Once the cumin seeds start to brown, add most of the onion (reserve some to sprinkle on the finished curry) and fry until translucent. Stir in the ginger, garlic, and chile and fry for a few seconds, then add the tomato passata or purée and cook for 1–2 minutes, until the oil separates from the sauce. Add the ground coriander, amchoor, ground cumin, turmeric, garam masala and chile powder and mix well. Season with sea salt. Cook for 2–3 minutes, adding a few spoonfuls of the chickpea cooking water if it starts to get dry.

Ladle the chickpeas into the pan using a slotted spoon, adding as much of the chickpea cooking water as you like to reach your desired consistency for the curry. Mix everything together and simmer for about 10 minutes.

Serve topped with a sprinkling of garam masala and some raw chopped onion and cilantro, alongside rice or flatbread.

TIP

If you can't find some of the spices, such as asafetida and amchoor, it is okay to omit. The result is just as delicious.

THE
GOOD
EGG

EGGS GIVE LIFE.

They symbolize fertility and rebirth, long life, and even immortality. Indeed, eggs are invincible—an egg in the fridge is the gateway to a certain quick and deeply satiating meal. Eggs featured heavily on our family table growing up. My mother made the most wonderful fried eggs in her beloved wok, with crispy edges and soft, gooey yolk centers. This egg, draped over white rice, with a simple drizzle of soy sauce, was a meal we relished. Today, eggs have renewed currency—they are a humble pantry staple that can gracefully adapt to diverse dishes and manifold cuisines. From Mexican chilaquiles to Turkish *menemen*, from Middle Eastern and North African baked eggs to Burmese egg curry, eggs are mild-mannered culinary globe-trotters that steadfastly shine on the plate.

TURKISH MENEMEN WITH CAVOLO NERO

Serves 4 / gluten free

Eggs are my favorite "breakfast-for-dinner" meal. *Menemen*, a Turkish-style scrambled egg dish cooked with tomato, bell pepper and spices, is right up there as one of the great breakfast egg meals, alongside huevos rancheros, chilaquiles, and shakshuka. This dish is intense and so full of flavor, but uses everyday ingredients you will find in your fridge. Slow and steady is the trick with menemen—stir the eggs gently to allow them to cook evenly while still maintaining distinct sections of yolk and white. The traditional recipe does not include greens, but I just love cavolo nero (lacinato kale) or curly kale with my eggs. And I've also included the tiniest pinch of saffron, which really takes this dish to another level. All you need is some crusty bread or flatbread to mop up the sauce.

6 large eggs
½ teaspoon dried chile flakes
tiny pinch of saffron, soaked in
   1 tablespoon of hot water for
   10 minutes
extra-virgin olive oil
1 garlic clove, crushed
1 small red onion, finely diced
1 large red bell pepper, seeded
   and finely chopped
5½ ounces (150 g) cavolo nero leaves,
   roughly chopped
4 tomatoes (about 14 ounces/400 g),
   diced
4½ ounces (120 g) feta, crumbled
handful of flat-leaf parsley leaves,
   finely chopped
sea salt and black pepper
crusty bread or sourdough loaf,
   to serve (optional)

Substitute

cavolo nero: spinach, chard, kale
fresh tomatoes: 1 can of diced tomatoes

Break the eggs into a bowl, season with sea salt and black pepper, then add the chile flakes and the saffron with its soaking water. Beat very gently, just enough to break up the yolks—you want the yolks and whites to remain mostly separate. Set aside.

Heat some olive oil in a large frying pan over a medium heat. Add the garlic and red onion, along with a pinch of sea salt and cook for 3–4 minutes, or until the onion is soft. Add the bell pepper and cook, stirring occasionally, for 7–8 minutes, until softened.

Add the cavolo nero and diced tomatoes to the onion and bell pepper mixture, along with a big pinch of salt and pepper. Cook for 2–3 minutes to allow the tomato to break down. When fragrant and thickened, very slowly stir in the beaten egg and cook for 1–2 minutes, until just set.

To serve, spoon the egg onto plates and top with the crumbled feta and a generous scattering of parsley. Serve with crusty bread or a sourdough loaf, if you like.

MY MOTHER'S STIR-FRIED TOMATO AND EGG

Serves 4 / gluten free

When I ring my mother from New York on the landline—and not on the usual FaceTime, which is her time to see the kids—she knows that I'm calling for a recipe. She answers the phone with glee, as there is nothing she loves more than telling me how to cook. This is her tomato and egg "stew." In truth, it is weird. First of all, because Cantonese don't eat a lot of tomatoes. And then to team it with eggs. And then add sugar. The mind boggles. But somehow, amidst the discordant flavor profiles, it works. This dish is the epitome of Cantonese home-style cooking and almost every family has their own version.

4 tomatoes (about 1 ⅓ pounds/600 g)
extra-virgin olive oil
¾-inch (2 cm) piece of ginger, peeled and finely chopped
3 tablespoons brown sugar
4 large eggs, lightly beaten
3 scallions, finely chopped
sea salt and white pepper
cooked white rice, to serve

Set up a large bowl with ice and cold water—this is your ice bath for peeling the tomatoes. Boil a pot of water. Using a sharp paring knife, mark a small "x" at the bottom of each tomato and add them to the boiling water. The skin will wrinkle and split—this should take 60–90 seconds. Remove from the water and drop them straight into the ice bath. Once the tomatoes are cool, lift them out of the water and peel away the skin. Chop the tomato flesh.

Add some oil to a saucepan, along with the chopped tomatoes and ginger, and stir well. Cover and cook over a medium–low heat for 5 minutes. Add the brown sugar and a splash of water, cover again, and cook for another 2 minutes.

Lightly season the beaten egg with a little sea salt and a small pinch of white pepper.

Increase the heat for the tomato mixture to high and very slowly trickle the beaten egg into the tomato mixture, allowing the heat to cook the egg. Once the egg has set into solid pieces, stir gently to break them up a little. Taste and season with sea salt.

Top the stir-fried tomato and egg with the chopped scallions and serve with white rice.

TIPS

If you don't have fresh tomatoes, you can use canned peeled tomatoes.

The more traditional way of preparing this dish is to scramble the eggs separately and then mix with the tomato sauce. You can try this if you prefer the egg to be more "solid."

CHILAQUILES WITH BAKED EGGS

Serves 4 / gluten free

On a recent family holiday to Playa del Carmen, we became enamored with the Mexican breakfast classic chilaquiles. When we came home, I swiftly added chilaquiles to our dinner roster—it is now on high rotation around our table. The fried tortillas start off crispy, but as they thirstily slurp up the spiced salsa verde, they transform into the most delicious sloppy corn chips you've ever tasted! You can use tomatoes in place of tomatillos, but you may want to add more citrus (lime) to inject some tartness. The baked eggs are my own touch, adding a fortifying heartiness. I've also included a list of recommended toppings, but you can top with whatever textural add-ons you like.

extra-virgin olive oil
1½ cups (375 ml) vegetable stock
4–6 large eggs
sea salt

SALSA VERDE
extra-virgin olive oil
1 red onion, roughly chopped
1 garlic clove, roughly chopped
1 pound (450 g) tomatillos
    (or tomatoes), roughly chopped
½ jalapeño chile, roughly chopped
    (optional)
1 bunch of cilantro, leaves picked
juice of ½ lime
sea salt and black pepper

FRIED TORTILLAS
vegetable or sunflower oil
15–20 fresh corn tortillas, each cut
    into 8 wedges
sea salt

TOPPING RECOMMENDATIONS
black beans
cilantro leaves
corn kernels
crème fraîche
crumbled feta
sliced cucumber

To make the salsa verde, heat a saucepan over a medium–high heat. Once hot, add a drizzle of olive oil and the red onion, garlic, chopped tomatillo and jalapeño, along with 2 tablespoons of water. Bring to the boil, then reduce the heat to low and cook for about 10 minutes, stirring often, until everything is very soft. Place the tomatillo mixture in a blender or food processor and add the cilantro leaves, along with a big pinch of sea salt and black pepper. Blend until smooth. Taste and season with more salt, if needed, and a squeeze of lime juice. Set aside.

For the fried tortillas, add a few tablespoons of oil to a large, deep frying pan and heat until it is very hot (you could also use a deep-fryer or wok). Reduce the heat to medium and fry the tortilla wedges, working in batches, turning them so that both sides are golden and crisp. Transfer to a paper towel to drain and immediately sprinkle with sea salt. Continue to cook in the same way, until all the tortillas have been fried.

In a large frying pan, add a drizzle of olive oil, along with the salsa verde and vegetable stock. Stir and bring to a simmer. Add the fried tortilla chips, turning them to coat the chips in the sauce. Once everything is well mixed, make a well near the side of the pan and break an egg directly into it. Repeat with the remaining eggs, working your way around the pan. Scatter everything with a little sea salt, cover with a lid, and cook over a gentle heat for 6–8 minutes, until the egg whites are just set and the yolks are still runny.

To serve, spoon the chilaquiles and baked eggs onto individual plates and serve with your selection of toppings.

TIPS

Cooled salsa verde can be stored in the fridge in a clean, sterilized container for up to 2 weeks.

If you're short on time, here are two great shortcuts—use good-quality store-bought corn chips and salsa verde, jazzing up the jarred sauce with some lime juice and finely chopped cilantro.

EGG SALAD WITH CHARRED ASPARAGUS AND POPPYSEED CHICKPEAS

Serves 4 / gluten free

Add an egg salad to your repertoire for endless possibilities. The crispy, just-tender asparagus is dreamy next to the richness of eggs. I serve egg salad with veggies often—we enjoy it with Brussels sprouts (highly recommend!) and often devour it alongside kale or broccoli. Egg salad is also delicious in its natural habitat, a sandwich.

1 large bunch of asparagus
(about 1 pound/450 g),
woody stems removed
extra-virgin olive oil
2 teaspoons poppy seeds
9 ounces (250 g) cooked chickpeas
(about 1 drained can)
juice of ½ lemon
chopped chives (optional)
sea salt and black pepper

EGG SALAD

5 hard-boiled large eggs, peeled
⅓ cup (80 g) good-quality mayonnaise
¼ teaspoon paprika
1 teaspoon Dijon mustard
2 teaspoons chopped chives
sea salt and black pepper

Substitute

asparagus: green beans

Drizzle the asparagus with olive oil. Heat a grill or grill pan until very hot and add the asparagus. Grill, turning often, for 2–3 minutes, until the spears are nicely charred but still crunchy and bright green. Remove from the pan and season with sea salt and black pepper. Set aside.

Place a frying pan over a medium–high heat. Add the poppy seeds and fry for 30 seconds, until fragrant. Drizzle the poppy seeds with olive oil and add the chickpeas, along with a big pinch of sea salt. Cook for 3–4 minutes, until the chickpeas have taken on some color. Remove from the heat and squeeze over the lemon juice.

To make the egg salad, mash the hard-boiled eggs with the back of a fork. Add the mayonnaise, paprika, mustard, and chives, and season with sea salt and black pepper.

Place the asparagus on a serving platter and pile the chickpeas on top. Drizzle with olive oil and season with sea salt and black pepper. To serve, dollop a big spoonful of egg salad on the side and scatter with chives, if using.

CHICKPEA, KALE, AND FETA STEW WITH ZA'ATAR BAKED EGGS

Serves 4 / gluten free (with rice)

This bake is inspired by my favorite "breakfast-for-dinner" dish, shakshuka. In Israel, shakshuka is an intense and spicy start to the day, but everywhere else, we have adopted shakshuka for breakfast, brunch, lunch, and dinner. This is a truly adaptable one-pan dish. My rendition starts off as a rich chickpea and kale stew, spiced with ground cumin, coriander, paprika, and nutmeg; eggs are then nestled in and around the stew and baked until just set. I like the yolks still runny, but cook a little longer if you prefer firmer yolks. This stew can also be enjoyed without the eggs or feta, for a quick vegan dish.

extra-virgin olive oil
1 yellow onion, finely chopped
2 garlic cloves, finely chopped
1 teaspoon ground cumin
1 teaspoon ground coriander
1 teaspoon paprika
½ jalapeño chile, seeded and
   finely chopped
18 ounces (500 g) cooked chickpeas
   (about 2 drained cans)
14 ounces (410 g) diced tomatoes
   (about 1 can)
½ cup (125 ml) vegetable stock
½ bunch of kale, stems removed
1 cup (150 g) feta, crumbled
4–6 large eggs
1 tablespoon za'atar
handful of mint leaves
sea salt and black pepper
rice or pita bread, to serve
Greek yogurt, to serve

Substitute

omit eggs and feta for vegan

Preheat the oven to 400°F (200°C).

In a deep ovenproof frying pan or Dutch oven, heat a drizzle of oil and add the onion and garlic. Cook for 3–4 minutes, until the onion is translucent, then add the cumin, coriander, paprika, and jalapeño, stirring for 30–60 seconds to allow the spices to release their flavors.

Add the chickpeas, tomatoes, and stock to the pan and stir to combine. Cover with a lid and cook for 15 minutes, until the sauce has thickened slightly. Season with sea salt and black pepper. Add the kale, cover, and cook for another 2 minutes, until the kale is wilted. Sprinkle the feta over the sauce and, one at a time, make little wells in the stew—making sure to space them out evenly—and break the eggs directly into them. Sprinkle the eggs with za'atar. Cover, transfer to the oven, and bake for 6–8 minutes, until the whites are set but the yolks are still runny.

To serve, scatter over the mint and finish with a sprinkle of sea salt and a drizzle of oil. Place the stew in the middle of the table and eat with rice or pita bread, alongside a dollop of Greek yogurt.

TIP

The stew can be made up to 2 days ahead and kept in the fridge until ready to eat. Break the eggs in and bake just before eating.

GOLDEN EGG CURRY

Serves 4 / gluten free (with rice or quinoa)

Variations of egg curry are pervasive throughout Asia—there are son-in-law eggs from Thailand (fried hard-boiled eggs in tamarind sauce), sweet-and-sour eggs from Malaysia and many egg curry dishes from Indonesia, India, Bangladesh, and Pakistan. Golden egg curry is Burmese in origin and is traditionally made with duck eggs. My take on this dish is loosely inspired by the warming spices of golden milk. Turmeric, cinnamon, and ginger join to create a richly spiced curry. This dish is elevated by hearty hard-boiled eggs, which are fried in turmeric-laced oil.

8 large eggs
⅓ cup (80 ml) vegetable oil
1 teaspoon ground turmeric
  (or 2 teaspoons grated fresh turmeric)
2 shallots, halved lengthwise and sliced
1 garlic clove, finely chopped
½ teaspoon ground cinnamon
¾-inch (2 cm) piece of ginger, peeled and finely chopped
½–1 jalapeño or long green chile, seeded and sliced lengthwise into strips
4 large tomatoes, finely chopped
2 scallions, finely sliced
sea salt and black pepper
rice, quinoa, or flatbread, to serve

Place the eggs in a saucepan and cover with cold water. Bring to the boil, reduce the heat to medium, and boil for 8 minutes. Drain the eggs and run under cold running water. When cool enough to handle, peel the eggs.

Add the oil to a frying pan, along with the turmeric. Heat until very hot (test with a wooden chopstick or wooden spoon; if it sizzles, the oil is ready). Slowly add the peeled eggs and fry, turning with chopsticks or a spoon, until blistered and golden all over. Remove the eggs from the oil and set aside. Discard the oil and wipe the pan clean.

In the same pan, drizzle a little oil and set over a medium heat. Once hot, add the shallots and garlic and season with some sea salt. Cook for 2–3 minutes, until the shallots have softened. Add the cinnamon, ginger, and chile and cook for another 1–2 minutes to release the flavors, then add the tomatoes, along with a splash of water, and season with sea salt and black pepper. Simmer for 10–15 minutes, until the tomato has broken down—if the mixture gets dry, add a little more water.

Cut each egg in half lengthwise and place, cut-side down, into the sauce. Turn up the heat and cook for 3–4 minutes, until the sauce is thick and bubbling.

Top the egg curry with a sprinkle of sliced scallions and serve with rice, quinoa, or flatbread.

SWEET TALKING

SWEETS ARE SURRENDER.

No matter how replete you feel, there is always room for dessert. Rarely a dish that we "need," dessert is sweet surrender, giving in to our most basic instincts. Dessert is aspirational, the optional-yet-essential part of the meal that indulges all our senses. While many desserts can be epic to produce, requiring many hours of precision, the best sweets are the ones with familiar flavors and simple baking techniques that families can cook together, time and time again. My favorite desserts are always rustic country-style sweets like puddings, dumplings, crumbles, and pies—heirloom recipes and memorable treats that are shared from one generation to the next.

THE PORTUGUESE WAY, WITH MARIA MIDOES

MARIA CELEBRATING HER FIRST BIRTHDAY WITH HER MUM.
PHOTOGRAPH CAPTURED BY HER MATERNAL GRANDFATHER.
CALDAS DA RAINHA, PORTUGAL, JULY 1985.

(OPPOSITE) MARIA, HER HUSBAND DIOGO, AND HER DOG KIKA,
AT HOME IN BROOKLYN.

There is something very raw about Maria Midoes's connection with food. It is like food sustains her, not only physically, but mentally and emotionally.

The first time I met Maria, I cooked her a kale Caesar salad, and as she took her first bite, she looked at me, watery eyed, and said it reminded her of the salads her mother used to make. Since that day, Maria and I have shared many salads, and every time we do, she has brought her bright smile and evocative love of food to the table.

Maria's childhood is a tale of two towns in her native Portugal, only 17 miles (28 km) apart but culturally disparate. The first is her father's hometown of Nazaré, a famous fishing village that is also home to some of the world's biggest surf waves. Further inland, there is the thermal spa town of Caldas da Rainha, her mother's hometown, where she moved after her parents separated. As Maria moved between her two homes, the table became an anchor where she experienced a strong sense of family and intimacy.

"My best memories are at the table, especially because my parents were divorced. On weekends, I would have lunch with my father and dinner with my mother—meals were a reason to be together. I believe it's a very Portuguese thing actually—it's more common in our culture to invite someone over to dinner than to go to the movies or for a walk."

As it turns out, traversing two towns with contrasting landscapes and lifestyles gave Maria a unique opportunity to connect with the diverse, rich food history of both sides of her family.

"I was very lucky because my father's side of the family always lived by the sea—my grandfather was a fishmonger, so my grandmother cooked fish with her eyes closed. My mother's parents used to have a farm where they kept poultry, pigs, and ducks. In terms of food influences, this was massive because I was able to learn completely different recipes from both sides of the family."

In Maria's home, food is strongly linked to emotions: "My grandmother on my father's side lost a son forty years ago. When that happened, she stopped cooking desserts because she felt like there was no reason to celebrate. She only started cooking desserts again six or seven years later after her first grandson was born. If my mum was sad, I would cook for her. Food for my family was always linked with emotion, care, devotion, and love for the ones sitting with us."

Cooking with her mother, laughing with her in the kitchen, and shopping together for produce, provided Maria with a feeling of safety. It was in these simple familial moments that her deep-rooted love for culinary storytelling would grow and flourish.

Maria's most treasured recipe is her mother's pear tart, a recipe that—until the photo shoot for this book—she had cooked often but never actually tasted (because she doesn't like butter!). With her mother's passing in 2014, this recipe would become crucial in keeping beloved memories alive.

"My mum's pear tart was her signature dessert. Even though I had never tasted it, the smell in the kitchen is a memory that never goes away. We used to go to the market together to choose the pears (or apples). Every time I cook it, I close my eyes and the smell around me is the closest thing to hugging her again. So to me, it's the most important recipe I can ever make—it's our way of meeting each other."

After finally trying her mum's pear tart, for the very first time, Maria now understands why this dessert was so loved by so many of her mum's friends.

MAMI'S PEAR TART

Recipe by Maria Midoes

Serves 8

If preparing the pears beforehand, make sure you keep them in water, with a squeeze of
lemon juice added, to stop them from oxidizing and turning brown.

1–2 pears, skin on, thinly sliced
confectioners' sugar, to dust (optional)

CRUST

2 cups (300 g) all-purpose flour
½ cup (1 stick; 115 g) good-quality
   unsalted butter, at room temperature,
   cut into small pieces
pinch of sea salt
pinch of ground cinnamon
1 large egg

FILLING

1 cup (230 g) superfine sugar
3 large eggs
6 tablespoons (90 g) good-quality,
   unsalted butter, melted
2–3 pears, peeled and thinly sliced

Preheat the oven to 400°F (200°C). Grease a 9-inch (23 cm) loose-bottomed tart pan.

For the crust, place the flour and butter in a large bowl. Rub the butter into the flour until
it is a sandy consistency. Add the salt and cinnamon and mix well, then add the egg and
mix with your hands until the dough comes together. Press the dough into the base
and side of the prepared tart pan, place it in the oven, and bake for 5–6 minutes, until
lightly golden. Remove and set aside to cool slightly.

For the filling, whisk together the sugar and eggs until combined. Add the melted butter
and beat with an electric mixer until the mixture is smooth. Using a spoon, fold in the
peeled and sliced pears.

Pour the filling into the tart shell and arrange the unpeeled sliced pears on top. Bake for
about 30–40 minutes, until golden and firm. Remove the tart from the oven and leave to
cool for about 30 minutes. To serve, dust with confectioners' sugar, if you like.

CHOC—ORANGE SELF-SAUCING PUDDING

Serves 6

This recipe belongs to my mother-in-law, Theresa McKinnon. Theresa bakes the old-fashioned way—with simple ingredients and humble flavors. These are modest desserts that would, back in the day, efficiently feed her nine children! Her dessert recipes are an homage to Australian country baking, clever little gems that never fail to impress. This self-saucing pudding is one of her best. How does a pudding self-sauce? The process is a little strange—cake batter, topped by a layer of sugar and cocoa, followed by boiling water—but trust it. Through alchemy, chemistry, or just plain magic, the flour rises to the top and the heavier sauce falls to the bottom. Simple. And simply incredible.

½ cup (125 ml) milk

1 large egg

5 tablespoons (75 g) unsalted butter, melted and cooled

1 tablespoon orange juice

zest of 1 orange

1 teaspoon vanilla extract

1 cup (150 g) self-rising flour (to make your own, see recipe tip on page 166)

2 tablespoons cocoa powder

½ cup (115 g) brown sugar

berries, to serve

whipped cream or vanilla ice cream, to serve

CHOCOLATE SAUCE

2 tablespoons cocoa powder

¾ cup (165 g) brown sugar

1¼ cups (310 ml) boiling water

Substitute

brown sugar: superfine sugar

Preheat the oven to 350˚F (180˚C). Grease a 6-cup (1.5 liter) pudding steamer, Pyrex bowl, or baking dish.

In a medium bowl, lightly whisk together the milk, egg, melted butter, orange juice, orange zest, and vanilla extract until well combined.

Sift the flour and cocoa powder into a large bowl and stir in the brown sugar. Add the milk mixture to the dry mixture and gently fold together until everything is combined and smooth. Spoon the batter into the prepared pudding steamer, bowl, or baking dish.

For the chocolate sauce, combine the cocoa powder and brown sugar and sprinkle this over the pudding. Very slowly, pour the boiling water over the back of a large metal spoon over the pudding (this helps the water land more gently, without disturbing the batter).

Bake for 30–35 minutes, until the pudding bounces back when pressed in the center.

To serve, scoop a big spoonful of pudding into a bowl and top with berries and a dollop of whipped cream or vanilla ice cream.

TIP

If you don't like orange, simply omit the zest and juice. No other changes necessary.

CHOCOLATE AND CHERRY SEMIFREDDO

Serves 6-8 / gluten free

I first tried semifreddo at an Italian cooking class in Sydney. It was espresso flavored and it floored me. This chocolate and cherry semifreddo is one that I often make for family celebrations. In Sydney, I usually served it at Christmas time, when cherries are in season. The joy in semifreddo is in its fluffy, soft texture. In Italian, semifreddo means "half cold," which is a perfect description for this mousse-like ice cream that remains velvety, even straight out of the freezer. The mixture is whipped, so it contains a lot of air and sugar, which keeps it from becoming too hard. Better still, no ice cream churner required!

9 ounces (250 g) cherries, pitted (fresh, frozen, or drained jarred Morello cherries are fine), plus extra to serve
¾ cup (170 g) superfine sugar, divided
1½ cups (375 ml) heavy cream
6 large egg yolks
½ cup (125 ml) milk
11 ounces (300 g) dark chocolate, melted and cooled

Line a loaf pan—about 8-10 inches (20–25 cm) long is best—with plastic wrap, making sure there is enough overhang on all sides to fold over the top of the semifreddo.

Place the cherries and ½ cup (115 g) of the superfine sugar in a saucepan and simmer over a low heat, stirring, for 3 minutes, or until the sugar dissolves. The cherries will release some of their juices. Remove from the heat and allow the cherry syrup to cool.

Whip the cream until soft peaks form. Place in the fridge to chill until required.

Beat the egg yolks in an electric mixer on medium speed for 4–5 minutes, until thick and creamy.

Meanwhile, heat the milk and the remaining ¼ cup (55 g) of sugar in a small saucepan over low heat, stirring, until the sugar dissolves. Bring to a simmer, then remove from the heat. With the mixer motor running on the lowest setting, very slowly trickle the milk mixture into the beaten egg yolks. Increase the speed to medium and continue to beat for about 4–5 minutes, until the mixture is fluffy and cold (feel the bottom of the bowl to gauge whether the mixture is cold).

Stir the cooled melted chocolate into the mixture, then gently fold in the softly whipped cream until it is all combined. Don't stir or fold too vigorously, as you want the mixture to stay light and airy.

Fold half of the cherry syrup into the chocolate mixture. Spoon the rest of the cherry syrup over the base of the loaf pan, then pour the chocolate mixture over the top. Smooth the top with a spatula, cover with the overhanging plastic wrap, and place in the freezer overnight or until firm.

To serve, cut into thick slices and serve with extra cherries.

TIPS

Swap out the chocolate for puréed fruit such as raspberries and strawberries. You can also replace the chocolate with 3 tablespoons of brewed espresso coffee mixed with 2 tablespoons of strong instant coffee granules.

The semifreddo can be made a week in advance (or longer).

This semifreddo contains raw eggs, so avoid serving to those who shouldn't eat raw eggs!

ANY FRUIT CRUMBLE

Serves 10 / gluten free

Fruit crumbles are one of the best ways to showcase seasonal fruits. Hence, I developed my "any fruit" crumble to allow you to use your favorite seasonal produce. Wonderful fillings include apple and rhubarb (my fave), mixed berries, cherry with chocolate, and pear with ginger, while during the summer months, peach with blueberry is my obsession. Any fruit works. The only thing to remember is to manage the liquid. Some fruits, like berries, will break down faster and emit lots of juice; cook these minimally, or even dust them in some tapioca flour before cooking to thicken up the syrup. Apples and pears will take longer to cook, so vary your cooking times accordingly. For berries, I would cook 3–5 minutes, for apples and pears, closer to 20. If you are using a tart fruit like rhubarb, don't add too much lemon juice. I recommend adding a spice to your filling; cinnamon is nice with apple, ginger is great with pear, and lemon zest works well with berries.

COCONUT CRUMBLE

1 cup (100 g) almond meal

⅔ cup (65 g) unsweetened or shredded coconut

½ cup (115 g) brown sugar

½ cup (90 g) brown or white rice flour

½ cup (1 stick; 115 g) unsalted butter, melted

3 tablespoons slivered almonds

FRUIT FILLING

3 tablespoons (45 g) unsalted butter

1 cup (100 g) superfine sugar

5 cups (750 g) fruit, cut into chunks

1 teaspoon vanilla extract

squeeze of lemon juice

vanilla ice cream or whipped cream, to serve

Preheat the oven to 350°F (180°C). Grease a 9-inch (23 cm) loose-bottomed tart pan.

For the coconut crumble, place the almond meal, coconut, brown sugar, and rice flour in a bowl. Pour in the melted butter and stir until combined.

Reserving about a third of the crumble mixture for topping, pour the rest into the prepared pan and press it into the base. Bake for 10 minutes, until lightly golden. Remove from the oven and set aside. Maintain oven temperature.

To make the fruit filling, melt the butter together with the sugar in a saucepan over a medium heat. When the butter has melted, add the fruit, along with the vanilla and a touch of lemon juice, cover with a lid, and cook over a low heat for 3–20 minutes, depending upon your fruit—apples and pears may take up to 20 minutes to soften, while berries will only take 3–5 minutes to start breaking down. Once the fruit is soft, it's ready to go. Uncover and stir briefly, then leave to cook for a few more minutes, until the fruit mixture is thick and syrupy.

Add the slivered almonds to the reserved crumble mixture and toss to combine.

Spoon the fruit into the tart shell and sprinkle the reserved crumble mixture on top. Return to the oven and bake for another 15 minutes, until golden. Serve with vanilla ice cream or whipped cream.

TIPS

Make sure you peel fruits such as apples and pears before using.

Dust berries in tapioca flour or cornstarch before cooking to help thicken up the syrup.

BANANA GOLDEN SYRUP DUMPLINGS

Serves 4–5

Unlike many Australians, I did not grow up eating golden syrup dumplings. Dessert at my house was a pared-back affair—maybe a piece of fruit, or a few slices of orange. Perhaps it was this dessert-drought that made me into a non-dessert person. I can happily go days and days without eating anything sweet, but there are a few desserts that are my undoing. This is one of them. It was my husband, Ross, who first introduced me to these incredible pillowy sweet dumplings. He learned the recipe from his mum, who is really the queen of simple, minimal-effort, maximum-comfort desserts. These light and fluffy dumplings are perfect for soaking up the delicious sauce. My personal touch is the addition of banana, which amps up the caramel flavor.

1½ cups (150 g) self-rising flour
3 tablespoons (45 g) salted butter, at room temperature, cut into small pieces
1 large egg
⅓ cup (80 ml) milk
1 banana (about 4½ ounces/120 g), mashed
vanilla ice cream, to serve

SYRUP
3 tablespoons (45 g) butter
¾ cup (165 g) brown sugar
3 tablespoons golden syrup

Substitute
golden syrup: honey, maple syrup

Place the flour in a bowl and add the butter. Using your fingertips, rub the butter into the flour until the mixture has a coarse, sand-like consistency.

In a separate bowl, beat the egg together with the milk until combined, then stir in the mashed banana. Pour the egg mixture into the butter and flour mixture and stir together to make a wet dough.

To make the syrup, in a large wide saucepan, melt the butter over a low heat. Add the brown sugar, golden syrup, and 2 cups (500 ml) of water and stir until combined.

Bring the syrup to the boil, then use a tablespoon to drop a golf-ball–sized dumpling straight into the pan. Repeat until you have used all the dough— you should have around 8–10 large dumplings. Reduce the heat to low and simmer gently for 15 minutes, until the dumplings are puffed up and a skewer inserted into the center of one of them comes out clean.

To serve, place 1–2 dumplings in a small bowl alongside some vanilla ice cream. Top with some of the syrup from the pan and serve immediately.

TIP
The dumpling dough is best made just before serving.

Golden syrup has a thick, molasses-like consistency (without the molasses flavor). While it is common in Australia and the United Kingdom, it can be harder to come by in the United States. Look for a brand called Lyle's golden syrup which can be found online and at specialty grocery stores. A good substitute is maple syrup or even honey.

SWEET POTATO PIE

Serves 10

Autumn in America is pie season. Every year, we take a day trip to Upstate New York to pick our own apples, which we promptly turn into delicious homemade pies. While we are at the farms, we make sure to gorge on apple cider doughnuts, while nabbing every type of pie you could imagine from the onsite bakeries—cherry, pecan, peach, raspberry, banana cream, and more. Pumpkin pie is a stalwart during this season, but around our family table we prefer sweet potato pie. Boldly spiced with ground coriander, nutmeg, and cinnamon, this pie is creamy and wonderfully warming, yet light enough to come back for seconds.

SWEET POTATO FILLING

1 pound (450 g) sweet potatoes (about 2), peeled and cut into ½-inch (1 cm) chunks
¾ cup (165 g) brown sugar
1 teaspoon ground coriander
½ teaspoon freshly grated nutmeg
1 teaspoon ground cinnamon
¼ teaspoon salt
4 tablespoons (60 g) unsalted butter
1¼ cups (310 ml) evaporated milk
3 large eggs
1 teaspoon vanilla extract

WALNUT PIE CRUST

2 cups (200 g) walnuts
1 cup (150 g) all-purpose flour
2 tablespoons brown sugar
½ teaspoon salt
½ cup (1 stick; 115 g) chilled unsalted butter, cut into small pieces

cream or vanilla ice cream, to serve

Substitute

sweet potato: butternut squash

walnuts: almonds or hazelnuts

use gluten-free "cup for cup" flour mix for gluten free

Preheat the oven to 350°F (180°C). Grease a 9-inch (23 cm) loose-bottomed pie or tart pan.

For the walnut pie crust, in a food processor or blender, whiz together the walnuts, flour, brown sugar, and salt until fine. Add the butter and pulse again until the mixture forms a crumbly dough. Press this into the base and side of the prepared pan, then place this on a baking sheet and bake for 15–20 minutes, until lightly browned. Remove from the oven and let cool. Increase the oven temperature to 375°F (190°C).

To make the filling, place the sweet potato in a saucepan and add ½ cup (125 ml) of water. Cover and cook over a medium heat for 15–20 minutes, until the sweet potato is very soft. Drain.

Return the sweet potato to the saucepan, along with the brown sugar, coriander, nutmeg, cinnamon, salt, butter, and half the evaporated milk. Stir, and cook over medium heat for about 5 minutes. Using a food processor or blender, blend the sweet potato mixture until very smooth. Allow to cool.

Whisk the remaining evaporated milk together with the eggs and vanilla extract. Pour this egg mixture into the cooled sweet potato mixture and stir to combine.

Pour the sweet potato filling into the prepared pie crust, place on a baking sheet and bake for 10 minutes. Reduce the oven temperature to 325°F (165°C) and cook for a further 35–40 minutes, until the filling is cooked through and the center wobbles slightly when jiggled. Remove from the oven and leave to cool—it can be eaten warm, or at room temperature.

Serve each slice with a little cream or vanilla ice cream.

TIPS

This pie can be made the day before and stored in the fridge. Bring it back to room temperature before serving.

You can also make the pastry by hand. Buy pre-ground walnuts and just mix everything together in a bowl with a wooden spoon, then rub the butter into the nut mixture with your fingertips.

LIME PIE WITH ANZAC BISCUIT CRUST

Serves 6

This recipe is a tale of two allied desserts—America's key lime pie joins forces with Australia's buttery Anzac biscuits in a transcontinental dessert that really does it all! This pie is traditionally made with key limes, which originate from the Florida Keys and which are smaller than regular limes, with a higher acidity, stronger taste, and thinner rind. The first time I made this pie, I zested and juiced fiddly key limes for way too long! Now, I just use regular limes and the result is not quite as tart, but just as good. I use four egg yolks for extra creaminess, but you could use just three if you wanted to hold back on the richness (or use five yolks if you want it even more decadent!).

ANZAC BISCUIT CRUST

¾ cup (110 g) all-purpose flour
⅓ cup (80 g) brown sugar
¾ cup (70 g) rolled oats
½ cup (50 g) unsweetened or shredded coconut
1 teaspoon salt
5 tablespoons (75 g) salted butter
2 tablespoons golden syrup, maple syrup, or honey
½ teaspoon baking soda

LIME FILLING

1 tablespoon finely grated lime zest (from approximately 3 limes), plus extra to serve (optional)
4 large egg yolks
1 can (about 14 ounces/400 g) sweetened condensed milk
½ cup (125 ml) freshly squeezed lime juice (from about 12–15 key limes or 4–5 regular limes)

vanilla ice cream or whipped cream, to serve

Preheat the oven to 350°F (180°C). Grease a 9-inch (23 cm) pie pan.

For the Anzac biscuit crust, combine the flour, sugar, oats, coconut, and salt in a bowl. Melt the butter in a small saucepan over a medium–low heat. Once melted, add the golden syrup and baking soda—be careful as the mixture will foam—then add this to the dry ingredients and mix well to combine. Press the mixture into the base and side of the prepared pie pan. Use your fingertips or the base of a small cup to flatten out the base and side until it is thin and uniform (you may have too much biscuit crust—if so, roll the leftover mixture into 1-inch (2.5 cm) balls, flatten slightly and bake to make cookies). Bake in the oven for about 10–15 minutes, or until golden. Leave to cool. Maintain oven temperature.

To make the lime filling, place the lime zest in a bowl, add the egg yolks, and beat with a whisk or electric mixer until the mixture is pale, thick, and ribbony—this step is important, as having a smooth, thick mixture here will improve the overall texture of the pie. Add the condensed milk and beat again until well combined and thickened, then whisk in the lime juice.

Pour the filling into the cooled Anzac biscuit crust and return to the oven for another 10–15 minutes, until the filling has set but not browned on top. Leave the pie to cool completely before eating—I prefer to eat it chilled, so let it cool off in the fridge for 2–3 hours before devouring.

Serve with vanilla ice cream or whipped cream and a sprinkle of lime zest, if you like.

TIP

This pie will keep in the fridge for 5–7 days.

See page 261 for note about golden syrup.

ORANGE AND ROSEMARY OLIVE OIL CAKE

Serves 6–8

I have been baking olive oil cakes for years. I often make them for my kids' birthdays—they are excellent for rainbow layer cakes and sturdy for decorating, and they also freeze well. (I always have homemade cakes in the freezer for my kids' school lunches.) If you are a lazy baker like me, olive oil cakes are essential to have in your repertoire. Oil is much more forgiving than butter, and helps keep cakes moist. I like to use a fruity extra-virgin olive oil for a stronger taste, but use a lighter oil if you prefer. I adore the richness of this cake—the delicate savory undertones pair so elegantly with the herbaceous rosemary and zesty citrus. Feel free to omit the rosemary if you want a plainer finish. A simple yet impressive cake for all occasions.

1 cup (230 g) superfine sugar
zest and juice of 2 small oranges
2 tablespoons chopped rosemary leaves
2 large eggs, beaten
1 cup (250 g) Greek yogurt
1 cup (250 ml) extra-virgin olive oil
2 cups (250 g) self-rising flour
   (to make your own, see recipe tip on
   page 166)
confectioners' sugar, to dust

Substitute

orange: lemon or mandarin
extra-virgin olive oil: light olive oil,
macadamia oil, coconut oil

Preheat the oven to 325°F (160°C). Line a 9-inch (23 cm) springform pan with parchment paper.

Add the sugar, orange zest, and rosemary to a bowl and, using your fingertips, rub everything together until the sugar is fragrant and damp. Add the eggs and whisk until pale and thick. Beat in the yogurt and orange juice, then gradually whisk in the olive oil.

Sift the flour into a large bowl so it's lovely and aerated. Slowly pour in the wet ingredients and, using a large spoon or spatula, gently fold everything together until just combined. Pour the batter into the prepared cake pan.

Bake for 45–50 minutes, until a toothpick inserted in the center of the cake comes out clean. Cool in the pan on a wire rack for 20 minutes, then invert the cake onto the rack to cool completely. When cool and ready to eat, dust with confectioners' sugar.

THE GREAT BAVARIAN BAKE OFF, WITH JANINE PHILLIPSON

JANINE ON HER SECOND BIRTHDAY, CELEBRATING WITH HER BUNDT-SHAPED
ANGEL FOOD CAKE, BAKED BY HER MUM, PICTURED.

(OPPOSITE) JANINE WITH HER HUSBAND CHRIS AND KIDS VIANNEY AND JAY,
AT HOME IN SYDNEY'S NORTHERN BEACHES.

Janine Phillipson is endowed with a very special legacy. She is the niece of a prize-winning baker. Before *The Great British Bake Off*, there was the "Apple-icious Bake-Off" at the Colborne, Ontario Apple Blossom Festival in 1990, where Janine's aunt, Freda Bryan, walked off with the prestigious top prize. She won the championship with her Bavarian apple torte.

This excellence in baking and cooking in Janine's family does not stop at Aunt Freda. Her family has a long and rich history of food, which has spanned many corners of the globe—Canada, England, and now Australia. With British parents, Janine and her two sisters grew up in Toronto, Canada, where their mother managed to keep their English ties alive via food—Sunday roast with potatoes, veggies, and Yorkshire pudding. In their home, food was pure and ingredients were handled with care and detail. Janine's mum, Anne, cooked in an honest way, using old-fashioned preserving techniques that would see the family through their long Canadian winters.

"My mum made everything from scratch, and often the ingredients were homemade, preserved, or picked from a local farm—canned tomatoes, beans, jams, and relishes. We had the "fruit cellar," a cold cement floor in our basement, lined with shelves my dad had installed, for all the jars and ingredients bought in season or in bulk. My mum often picked what was seasonal—by the bushel basket or quart basket—and then preserved it by either freezing (we had a huge chest freezer) or canning it. She would also use seasonal produce to make pies and jams, including her famous freezer strawberry jam (which I now make with my daughter, Vianney). As a kid, I topped and tailed more green and yellow beans than I care to recall."

There was great care in the way food was prepared in Janine's family. Sunday meal plans or menus for family gatherings were kept on the fridge at least a week before the event. Janine's mum, a fervent baker, routinely churned out much-loved comfort food such as coffee cake, fresh strawberry pie (fresh strawberries in jelly and pastry!), and lemon loaf. Despite these strong food influences, Janine left home without many culinary skills. This all changed when her mum gifted her a binder of recipes, labelled "the recipes you grew up with." For Janine, this was a turning point—learning to cook this collection of family recipes was a way to feel connected to her mum and her childhood.

One of the "recipes you grew up with" was Aunt Freda's award-winning Bavarian apple torte. Cooking this simple dessert recipe, which originated in a Kraft cooking booklet, has always been a family affair, the joy of baking it together as special as the moments eating it.

"When I was a child, my mum and aunt used to make this together every Monday by the dozen for a small restaurant just outside Toronto. My cousin and I still make it regularly, always to rave reviews!"

BAVARIAN APPLE TORTE

Recipe by Janine Phillipson

Serves 4–6

PASTRY BASE

8 tablespoons (115 g) unsalted butter,
    at room temperature
⅓ cup (80 g) superfine sugar
¼ teaspoon vanilla extract
1 cup (150 g) all-purpose flour

FILLING

9 ounces (250 g) cream cheese, at room
    temperature
3 tablespoons superfine sugar
1 large egg
½ teaspoon vanilla extract

TOPPING

⅓ cup (80 g) superfine sugar
1 teaspoon ground cinnamon
2 apples, peeled, and cored
3 tablespoons sliced almonds

Preheat the oven to 425°F (220°C). Grease the base and side of an 8-inch (20 cm) springform pan.

For the pastry base, cream the butter, sugar, and vanilla extract together using an electric mixer, until light and fluffy. Add the flour and beat to combine and form a dough. Press the dough onto the base and 1 inch (2.5 cm) up the side of the prepared pan.

To make the filling, combine the cream cheese with the sugar and mix together well. Add the egg and vanilla extract and mix well until combined. Pour this mixture into the pastry-lined pan.

For the topping combine the sugar and cinnamon in a large bowl. Cut the apples into slices—not too thin—and add these to the cinnamon sugar. Toss well to coat all the slices, then arrange the apple slices on top of the filling, starting from the outer edge and working around in a circle, slightly overlapping the slices as you go. Sprinkle any leftover cinnamon and sugar over the top together with the almonds.

Bake for 10 minutes, then reduce the oven temperature to 375°F (190°C) and bake for another 25 minutes, until the center is set. Remove from the oven and allow to cool slightly on a wire rack. Serve warm or leave to cool completely before serving.

ACKNOWLEDGMENTS

There is a great responsibility in writing recipes. In doing so, we are asking readers to trust us enough to cook and share our recipes on a daily basis. So, my deepest gratitude goes to all the home cooks from around the world who have welcomed my recipes into their kitchens over the past five years. I am so humbled by your belief in my food.

Thank you to my international book family at Prestel for bringing this story to the world. Thank you to the charming and classy Holly La Due—your friendship, optimism, and guidance have meant so much to me over the past few years, and I am beyond thrilled to be working with you and your team. Thank you also to Karen Farquhar and everyone at Prestel for welcoming me so warmly into your family.

To my Australian book family at Plum Books—thank you to my wonderful longtime publisher Mary Small, for giving me the freedom to tell my stories, for your trust, and support. Thank you to the unflappable Clare Marshall, and uber-talented Charlotte Ree—what a team! You guys make it happen, effortlessly and always with smiles on your faces. Thank you also to all the people behind the scenes at Pan Macmillan Australia, who hit the road to spread the word about my books.

Thank you to my book family. To Luisa Brimble, my most trusted partner-in-crime from the very beginning—your energy and warmth are infectious and inspire me endlessly. Thank you for bringing laughter and light into my life. Thank you to the ever-stylish Erika Raxworthy, for your poise and the effortless way in which you create such beauty on these pages. Thank you to Tiffany Iung, my charming, sandwich-slinging mate—you are my perfect kitchen companion and it is such a joy to cook alongside you. And huge thanks to Jill Fergus, for your magical helping hands in the kitchen.

Thank you to my extended book family—Daniel New, Simon Davis, Lauren Salkeld, and Makiko Katoh.

Thank you to the very fierce and delightful Judy Linden. I feel invincible knowing that you are in my corner.

Thank you to my friends who so graciously shared their family food stories with me. Big bear hugs and heartfelt gratitude to Julia Ostro, Maria Midoes, Erin Jang, Lisa Marie Corso, Chitra Agrawal, Janine Phillipson and Szeki Chan—thank you for trusting me with your precious family memories and recipes. Your stories are the beating heart of this book.

To Davida Sweeney, your friendship assures my sanity—thank you for always telling me both what I need to hear and what I want to hear (that is true friendship!). To Jennifer Wong, my oldest buddy, thank you for over half a lifetime of capers. And to Shirley Cai, my sister from another mother—you are the best and brightest, and I'm so lucky to learn from you.

Thank you to my Brooklyn crew for giving me a family a long way from home—Adrienne Voboril, CC Malerba, Maria Midoes, Ron and Leetal Arazi, Samantha Hillman, Lorraine Abela, and Sara Woster. To Jodi Moreno, my dear friend turned business partner—we have created such magic together in our little corner of Brooklyn. I am so grateful for your adventurous spirit and the great food you bring to my days.

To the talented makers, big and small, who keep the art of pottery alive—thank you to Robert Gordon Australia, Mud Australia, Sophie Harle, Ilona Glastonbury at Otti Made, and Karin Hossack for making the beautiful wares that bring my food to life. Thank you also to Staub USA for your continued support.

Thank you to my small Lui family and my larger McKinnon family, who generously and unequivocally support me in everything that I do.

To my stellar little family who are the loves of my life. To my taste-testers, Scout, Dash, and Huck, my shiny, happy people. It is such a thrilling adventure to be your mum—I am so lucky to wake up each morning to your delectable faces, to get to kiss your pillowy cheeks, to receive your cuddles, and to experience your humor. To my husband Ross, who is my best person, the most generous, patient, calm person I know—thank you for making me laugh each and every day for the past twenty-something years (and counting). You are still so rad.

This book is dedicated to my mum. For filling my childhood table with the most delicious memories. And for showing me that, to feed, is to love. It's really that simple.

HM

INDEX

© 2019 Hetty McKinnon
Photography copyright © 2019 Luisa Brimble
Endsheet images © 2019 Hetty McKinnon

Originally published by Pan Macmillan Australia Pty Limited, 2018

Prestel Verlag, Munich • London • New York 2019
A member of Verlagsgruppe Random House GmbH
Neumarkter Strasse 28 · 81673 Munich

Prestel Publishing Ltd.
14-17 Wells Street
London W1T 3PD

Prestel Publishing
900 Broadway, Suite 603
New York, NY 10003

Library of Congress Cataloging-in-Publication Data
Names: McKinnon, Hetty, author. | Brimble, Luisa, photographer.
Title: Family : new vegetarian comfort food to nourish every day / by Hetty
McKinnon ; photography by Luisa Brimble.
Description: New York : Prestel Publishing, [2019] | Originally published by
Pan Macmillan Australia Pty Limited, 2018.
Identifiers: LCCN 2018032533 | ISBN 9783791385426 (hardcover)
Subjects: LCSH: Vegetarian cooking. | LCGFT: Cookbooks.
Classification: LCC TX837 .M2424 2019 | DDC 641.5/636--dc23
LC record available at https://lccn.loc.gov/2018032533

A CIP catalogue record for this book is available from the British Library.

For Pan Macmillan:
Design: Daniel New
Edited: Simon Davis
Index: Clare Marshall
Photography: Luisa Brimble (with additional photography by Hetty McKinnon)
Food styling: Hetty McKinnon
Prop styling: Erika Raxworthy
Food preparation: Tiffany Jung and Hetty McKinnon

For Prestel:
Editorial direction: Holly La Due
Cover design: Makiko Katoh
Production: Karen Farquhar and Anjali Pala
Copyediting: Lauren Salkeld
Proofreading: Monica Parcell

ISBN 978-3-7913-8542-6

Printed and bound in China

www.prestel.com

Verlagsgruppe Random House FSC® N001967